The
SWAN

A Natural History

For Jean
my inspiration

The
SWAN
A Natural History

MALCOLM SCHUYL

Merlin Unwin Books

First published in Great Britain by Merlin Unwin Books, 2012
Text and photographs © Malcolm Schuyl, 2012

Merlin Unwin Books Ltd
Palmers House
7 Corve Street
Ludlow, Shropshire SY8 1DB   U.K.
www.merlinunwin.co.uk
email: books@merlinunwin.co.uk

The author asserts his moral right to be identified as the author of this work.
A CIP catalogue record for this book is available from the British Library.

ISBN 978-1-906122-40-9

Designed and set in Palatino by Merlin Unwin
Printed and bound by 1010 Printing International Ltd

Contents

Introduction   9

1. Swans around the World   13

2. Attraction between Man & Swans   29

3. Swan Biology   39

4. Swan Behaviour   75

5. Enemies of the Swan   117

6. Swan Domestication   125

7. Swan Upping   139

8. Language & the Swan   147

9. Swan as a Name or Symbol in Society   153

10. The Swan & Culture   165

11. Swans & the Law   191

12. Saving our Swans   199

Index   221

The silver swan, who living had no note,

When death approach'd, unlock'd her silent throat;

Leaning her breast against the reedy shore,

Thus sung her first and last, and sung no more.

Farewell, all joys; O Death, come close mine eyes;

More geese than swans now live, more fools than wise.

Orlando Gibbons

Introduction

Go to any lake or river, either in the town or the countryside, and the chances are that you will be able to see Mute swans. These large, white, aquatic birds are a common sight and have graced our waterways for centuries. With their long, elegantly curved necks, white plumage and orange beaks, they are instantly recognisable. They are universally accepted as symbols of beauty and, because they are generally approachable, we tend to treat them with great affection and respect.

Years ago, I remember seeing groups of people surrounded by laughing children feeding the swans on a local lake. I was struck by how beautiful the swans looked, gliding serenely over the water, without any apparent fear of those noisy crowds. Over the following months I started to take a few photographs but didn't know much about their natural history at all. I began to watch and feed them myself and, the more photographs I took, the more I wanted to know, and a passion for swans soon developed. Many years later, I can honestly say that this passion is as strong now as it was all those years and many thousands of photographs ago.

Man's relationship with the swan goes back thousands of years. Probably because of their aesthetic appeal, we have an enduring interest, almost an infatuation, with these birds. Paintings of Mute swans have even been found on the walls of Bronze

Age caves, and there are references to swans in Ancient Greek and Roman history. They are still very visible in our society today and we do not have to look far to see numerous references to the swan in books, music, poetry, stamps, art, Coats of Arms, business logos, astronomy, public houses and theatres to name but a few. Even technological inventions like automobiles, ships and aircraft have been named after the swan. The word 'swan' has also crept into our language, with the use of phrases such as 'swanning around' and the concept of the 'swansong'.

The swan is often used as a symbol of love and fidelity because of its long-lasting monogamous relationships. Its graceful gliding on the water has made it a universally-recognised symbol of beauty. Swans are also revered in many diverse religions and cultures and they bring a great deal of joy into our lives.

The swan we are most likely to see in the UK is the Mute swan, one of a handful of swan species found around the world. The Mute swan is the only one that breeds here naturally. It is Britain's largest bird and one of the heaviest flying birds in the world. The other white swans that may be seen in the UK during the winter months are the Whooper swan and Bewick's swan which migrate south from their usual sub-Arctic breeding grounds.

In the UK, the swan has a special significance because of its links with Royalty. It has been a royal bird since the twelfth century and was formally assigned Royal Status in the *Act of Swans 1482*. Today the Crown retains the right to ownership of all unmarked Mute swans in open water but the Queen only exercises her rights on certain stretches of the river Thames and its tributaries.

A swan preens itself gracefully. Its white, pristine appearance has made it symbolic of many virtues.

Swans were once kept in Britain in a semi-domesticated state as a source of food, usually in 'swanneries' associated with castles and monasteries. Roast swan was often on the menu of an important banquet but nowadays swans are protected by law and it is illegal to capture, injure or kill them.

Swans are easy enough to see, and they give the impression of having a peaceful and carefree existence. But all is not as it seems and they still need our help and care. Even though they are now protected, they still frequently suffer from their proximity to humanity; for example, some are deliberately killed or injured, they can ingest discarded plastic, suffer from the effects of pollution, become tangled up in fishing line or be attacked by dogs. In some countries, licences are issued so that swans can be hunted.

Swans are fascinating creatures and are superbly adapted to the environment in which they live and breed. We see swans and depictions of them all around us and often come into contact with them, but generally we know little about their natural history or their roots in our society. The aim of this book therefore is to provide some interesting, perhaps even surprising, information, in images as well as text, in the hope that the reader will have a better understanding of these truly beautiful creatures whose lives are so entwined with ours.

Go to any lake or river, either in the countryside or the town, and the chances are you will be able to see Mute swans.

CHAPTER ONE

Swans around the World

The Mute swan is native to the Northern Hemisphere, mostly in Europe and Asia, but can occasionally be found as far south as the Mediterranean and North Africa. Truly wild populations, such as those in the more northern parts of its range, are migratory, particularly when they are displaced by severe winter weather. In most places, especially where they come into frequent contact with people, they can be either sedentary or roaming in nature, moving short distances to better feeding places. Very harsh winters can see more significant movements, where the birds will seek out water that remains unfrozen. The Mute swan has been seen in 70 different countries and found breeding in 49 of them. On the whole it is a lowland bird, rarely occurring above 300m in altitude. There is also an argument, much debated, that the Mute swan should be considered as native to North America, because their fossils have been discovered in various parts of the USA.

The world population of wild Mute swans is about half a million, the majority of which are in the former Soviet Union. The largest single breeding colony is in the Volga Delta. There are about 25-30,000 Mute swans in the UK, with about 5,000 breeding pairs. There are also significant populations in Denmark, Germany, Poland, The Netherlands and other European countries. During harsh winters, some birds migrate to eastern England from Europe.

Populations of wild swans in Western Europe up to the 19th century were largely exterminated by hunting as they were eaten extensively and considered to be a delicacy. Fortunately, many semi-domesticated birds were kept by wealthy landowners during this time, and this fact, together with better protection for wild birds, allowed them to increase almost to their former numbers during the 20th century. More recently, during the 1960s and 1970s, numbers were once more significantly reduced due

'Farming' swans for food probably saved the wild population.

to lead poisoning as birds swallowed lead weights discarded by fishermen. After lead was replaced by less toxic materials, the number of swans again increased rapidly.

Throughout history, Mute swans have been kept in captivity as decoration for parks and ponds. Some of these birds inevitably escaped and formed naturalised wild colonies. This explains why small populations of Mute swans can now be found outside their normal range, in countries such as Australia, New Zealand and

Left: The Black swan, native to Australia.

Below: A Black-necked swan, found in South America.

South Africa. In Japan, most of the current population are introduced birds but occasionally wild birds do find their own way there from Asia. In the United States, Mute swans were introduced during the late 1800s, again mainly for their ornamental value. Numbers there have increased rapidly and to such an extent that they are now viewed by some as an invasive species causing significant environmental damage. There is much debate about culling the birds to keep their numbers under control.

The Whooper swan.

Swan Species and Taxonomy

The Mute swan was first defined scientifically by the German naturalist Johann Friedrich Gmelin in 1789 and given the Latin name *Anas olor*, but it was then transferred by Johann Matthäus Bechstein to the then newly-named genus Cygnus in 1803. Both Cygnus and olor mean 'swan' in Latin.

Above: The Trumpeter swan of North America.

To see where the swan fits within the animal world, we need to look at its taxonomy. Taxonomy is the science of classification of living things, and is derived from the Greek word 'taxis' meaning

order. Taxonomy is therefore the branch of biology concerned with grouping organisms together based on similarities in structure and origin. It helps us to see how living things are related and how they might have evolved.

Above: A Polish swan, with distinctive pinkish-grey beak and feet.

The taxonomic classification of swans is as follows:

KINGDOM: Animalia (Animals)
PHYLUM: Chordata (Animals with backbones or vertebrates)
CLASS: Aves (Birds)
Order: Anseriformes (Ducks, Geese and Swans)
Family: Anatidae
Subfamily: Anserinae
Genus: Cygnus (Swans)
Species: There are several living (or extant) species of swan, all of them in the Genus Cygnus, and these are:

The Mute Swan *(Cygnus olor)*, the common, temperate European and Asian species, with all-white plumage (feathers) and an orange and black beak. Because of its visibility in society and almost constant association with man, the Mute swan has also been historically referred to as the 'common' or 'tame' swan.

The Black Swan *(Cygnus atratus)*, native to Australia and introduced to New Zealand, with almost entirely black plumage (it has some white feathers on its wings which are visible when it flies) and a red beak.

The Black-necked Swan *(Cygnus melancoryphus)*, from South America and the Falkland Islands, has white plumage and a characteristic black neck. It is the smallest of the swans.

The Whooper Swan *(Cygnus cygnus)* from Europe and Asia, but breeds in subarctic areas. It has all-white plumage with a yellow and black beak.

The Trumpeter Swan (*Cygnus buccinator*), a North American swan similar to the Whooper Swan. It is the largest swan, with all-white plumage and a predominantly black beak.

The Tundra Swan (*Cygnus columbianus*), the smallest of the all-white swans. It also has white plumage and a yellow and black beak. In Europe, this swan is known as the Bewick's Swan and in North America it is sometimes called the Whistling Swan. They breed in the high arctic areas of Russia and North America. There is some debate about whether these swans constitute two (or more) separate species, or whether they are just different sub-species of the same swan.

There are also some references to 'other' swans such as Polish swans and Jankowski's swans; these are generally considered to be variations of existing species that may differ slightly based on genetics or geographical separation. Polish swans (page 20) are now known to be Mute swans with a genetic deficiency that causes the legs and feet to be pinkish-grey rather than black. These swans were given their name when they were first imported from the Polish coast to London around 1800 and given the latin name *Cygnus immutabilis* or Changeless swan because its cygnets are born white rather than grey and hence do not change in colour when they mature. The name is however somewhat inappropriate as these swans occur no more frequently in Poland than in other areas of Europe. Jankowski's swans are Tundra swans that live in the Far East and they are slightly larger than their American and European counterparts.

There is one other species of swan, the Coscoroba Swan from South America, but this is not considered by some to be a true swan. Although it too has all-white plumage, it is smaller and more goose-like in appearance than other swans and has been placed in a separate taxonomic group all of its own (the genus *Coscoroba* rather than *Cygnus*).

Swans do not interbreed between species in the wild, but in captive conditions it has been known – for example, Whooper swans have successfully bred with Trumpeter swans.

In Eastern Asia, there is a large bird called the Swan-goose (*Anser cygnoides*), but this is unmistakably a goose and not a swan, and is similar in appearance to the Greylag goose.

Over the years, many words have been used to describe a collection or group of swans, such as a flock, a herd (the noun most accepted nowadays), drift, lamentation, bevy, ballet, regatta, team and bank. The term 'fleet' has also been used to describe a group of swans in captivity. Because of their tendancy to fly in a V-formation, a group of swans in flight is often called a 'wedge'.

The Evolution of the Swan

One of the best ways to work out how swans have evolved is to look at fossil records. Fossils can give us a glimpse into the past, and help us to understand how animals once lived and how this may have affected the species that are present today. There is a good fossil swan record from most parts of the world and a number of prehistoric species have been identified.

Left: The South American Coscoroba swan, not classified as a true swan.

The evolution of the swan is difficult to trace accurately, but it is believed that a prehistoric bird called *Presbyornis* (derived from the Greek for 'elderly bird') was the ancestor of all modern swans and geese. Numerous fossils of this bird have been found in various locations in North America and Asia and these date back to the Oligocene epoch about 35 million years ago. It was a rather strange creature, best described as a cross between a duck, a flamingo and a goose. It had the head and beak of a duck, long flamingo-like legs and neck and probably filtered food from the water with its broad beak.

Fossils of the swan as we know it today, however, have been found around the world, including the USA, Europe, Asia and Australia, with possibly a dozen or so different species having been identified so far. The evidence suggests that modern swans evolved in Europe or Western Asia during the Miocene period about 5-23 million years ago.

It is not known when the southern hemisphere swans (the Black and Black-necked) split from their Eurasian origins to form separate species. The Mute swan is thought to be most closely related to the Black swan, because of its habit of carrying its neck curved rather than straight, its tendency to fluff-up its feathers and similarities with the beak. The Whooper, Tundra and Trumpeter swans, because of similarities in appearance (yellow/black beak and straight neck), distribution and breeding habits, probably evolved along a separate evolutionary line to the other swans.

Perhaps the most fascinating fossil is that of the Giant swan (which has been given the Latin name *Cygnus falconeri*) from Malta, thought to be about a third bigger than the present-day Mute swan. It is believed to have existed about one million years ago and, because of its size, was most likely flightless. Its disappearance was due to predation by large carnivores, competition or unfavourable climatic conditions. Another equally large fossil swan was discovered 500 miles east of New Zealand on the Chatham Islands and it was thought to have survived until the 16th or 17th century. It has been named the Pouwa swan, a Maori name, and it is thought to be the ancestor of the Black swan.

CHAPTER TWO

Attraction between Man & Swans

What is it about the swan? Why do we find such a familiar bird so attractive and compelling, to the extent that it is infused into so many aspects of our lives? Its influence on our society is perhaps greater than any other animal, and this bond between man and bird stretches far back in our history.

There are many reasons why the swan has captured our imagination over the centuries. Human beings have a tendency to anthropomorphise the creatures we see around us; to perceive various features of our own lives as being mirrored in the natural world. Some qualities we favour, such as in the swan, and we embrace them; those that have negative connotations, such as in the shark, we reject, or worse, persecute.

The three basic characteristics of colour, behaviour and shape are all equally important in understanding the strength of our attraction to the swan.

An adult male swan prepares to take off from the water.

Left: A pair of courting Mute swans mirror one another's movements in a 'dance of love'.

The swan is a very visible bird; it is easy to identify, partly because of its white colour, but also because it is large and relatively common. We do not have to look very hard or search very far to see one and so it frequently finds its way into our thoughts without us even trying. We traditionally associate white with purity, cleanliness and love. One of our customs is for brides to get married in white. And because of swans' tendency to stay together for life,

we see them as symbolising loyalty, fidelity and the strength of partnership.

A courting pair of swans will swim closely together, mimicking each other's movements, sometimes arching their long necks together to form the familiar heart shape, yet another symbol of love. On the other hand, the male will fiercely defend his territory and protect his family, strong and admirable behaviour that Man respects. A swan swimming slowly on calm water with a perfect reflection is seen as an image of serenity; beautiful and inspirational, perhaps even displaying regal qualities. When in flight, the swan's slow wing-beat is the epitome of calmness and control, in sharp contrast to that of most other birds. Groups of swans will often fly in formation, seen as a sign of co-operation.

The swan's long, graceful and slender s-shaped neck is one of its most distinguishing features, inspirational to artists and poets, especially when reflected in the water. Being associated with water also has cultural and religious significance: water is symbolic of creativity, emotion and intuition.

Historically, the swan also had an erotic connection: its long slender neck suggesting the generative power of the male, and the white, curved body symbolising the female.

The Mute swan was also regarded (and of course erroneously named) as being silent, and the idea of strength through silence has been epitomised in the swan.

Enigmatic, silent,
strong. A 'busking'
Mute swan (see
page 86).

Many birds and animals have one or more of these attributes, but the swan is unique in having so many of them. They are seen as commendable qualities and ones to which we aspire. The swan has long been considered a "royal" bird because of its association with the Crown, and thus was seen as conferring status and beauty to its owner and his lands. The swan therefore is also associated with rank and quality.

So the reasons for our attraction to and association with the swan are numerous. We associate positively with its colour and shape and see it exhibiting behaviour that we admire. It is a symbol of quality, a thing of beauty in its own right and a status symbol to enhance the aesthetic appeal of one's estate. It has also been a valuable source of food for centuries.

Paired for life: the Mute swan.

CHAPTER THREE

Swan Biology

Male swans are known as cobs and females as pens. They are similar in appearance, but the males are slightly larger and have a more pronounced knob (or berry) on top of their beak. Both sexes have dark legs and feet. A fully-grown male can weigh up to 15kgs, which makes them one of the heaviest flying birds in the world. Their wing-span can be up to 8 feet, and although difficult to measure accurately, it has been estimated that the Mute swan can fly at up to 50mph, making it also one of the fastest flying birds in the world.

Young swans are known as cygnets and typically have brownish feathers for the first year before developing the all-white plumage of an adult bird. In captivity, swans have been known to live up to 50 years of age but their lifespan is much reduced in the wild, where few will live beyond 10 years. Probably the world's oldest wild Mute swan, estimated to be 40 years old, was found dead in Denmark in 2009.

Swans have certain unique anatomical characteristics which enable them to master the challenging elements of water and air in which they live.

In common with other aquatic birds such as ducks and geese, swans have long bodies and short legs; with webbed feet sited at the back of the body and widely spaced apart. This is an ideal design for living on water as it allows the swan to keep its balance more easily at it moves through the water.

The webbed feet are leathery and have four toes, three facing forward and one back. They use these like paddles to swim, spreading the toes on the backstroke to maximize push; holding them together on the forward stroke to minimize resistance from the water. Although an efficient design for life on water, it is not ideal on land and swans look particularly ungainly when walking.

A wing-span of up to 8 feet.

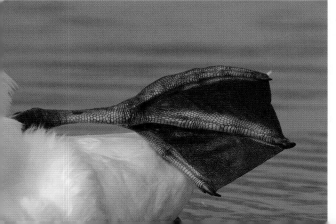

Three toes facing forwards, one back.

The swan's long neck is for under-water foraging and for ease of preening.

The long neck of the swan is an efficient design for getting the beak to places to feed, such as the bottom of a pond, without the need to submerge their whole body.

Like most birds, swans have evolved so that they can fly. There are two fundamental requirements that must be met in order to take to the air: low weight and high power. Birds have several unique adaptations which allow them to fulfil these basic needs. They have lightweight hollow bones, feathers and powerful wings, a strong heart and an efficient breathing system.

Skeleton

In order to reduce weight for flying (which, incidentally, also helps the birds float on water), they have fewer bones compared to a mammal or reptile. Many of their bones are hollow and thus are lighter. The heavy teeth and jaw bones of animals have been replaced by a much lighter beak and the larger limb bones have an internal support system of struts which makes them stronger.

The breastbone (or sternum) has evolved into a keel-shape which creates more surface area for the attachment of the larger breast muscles used for flying. Some of the hollow bones have air sacs that are connected to the lungs and respiratory system. The forelimbs have been modified to form wings and their natural movement is up and down, rather than back and forth as with other animals.

The skeleton of the swan is all about lightness and strength for flight.

44

The swan has more vertebrae than any other bird because of its long neck. Nevertheless the neck is strong and flexible, enabling it to forage effectively and to reach the oil gland at the base of its tail. This flexibility is also important in allowing the bird to turn its head to see better, as its eyes are fixed in deep sockets in the skull and therefore have very restricted movement (unlike our eyes).

Some of the lower vertebrae are fused to create a more stable frame when the bird is flying. The two collarbones are also fused to make what we call the wishbone (also called the furcula) which helps strengthen the ribcage. Flying creates a lot of stress on the skeleton so these adaptations for strength are very important in a heavy bird when taking to the air.

Despite being one of the heaviest birds to fly, the Mute swan is perfectly designed for this purpose.

Feathers

The second major adaptation that birds have is that of feathers. They are one of their most obvious features and unique to them – no other animal has them. Feathers perform several vital functions:

● they keep birds warm. From an evolutionary point of view, it is thought that feathers were initially developed for this purpose rather than to enable birds to fly. Birds are warm-blooded and it is essential they are protected from the cold. Feathers can be fluffed-up to trap air between them and these air pockets keep the birds warm, or alternatively air can be eliminated to help them cool down.

● they protect the body from water, especially important when living in an aquatic environment. Swans can make their feathers waterproof by covering them with oil gathered from a gland (the uropygial gland) at the base of the tail.

● they protect the bird's skin from a range of parasites etc, and from ultraviolet light to prevent sunburn.

● feathers are, of course, fundamental in enabling birds to fly. The ability to take to the air, originally by simply gliding rather

Using oil from the preen gland, the swan keeps its feathers extremely water-resistant.

than flying, provided the evolutionary pressure to develop a greater variety of feathers, stronger and more specialised, to enable birds to master proper flight.

- feathers can provide certain birds with camouflage

Swans, like other birds, have several different types of feathers, such as

- flight feathers on the wings and tail – these are strong, long and wide with a broad shaft and are used for flight

- soft and fluffy down feathers with little or no shaft, used for insulation by trapping air

- filoplume feathers, which are very small, are attached to nerve endings so that the bird can sense if they are misaligned in terms of feather placement – so vital for flying and insulation

- semiplume feathers are like a cross between flight and down feathers and are used for insulation

A feather is a dead structure made of a protein called keratin. While they are growing, feathers have a blood supply but this dries up once they are fully grown.

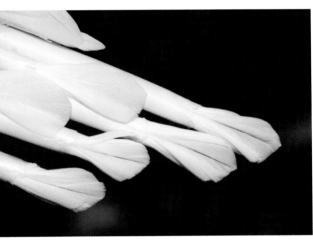

Top: growing feathers still showing the blood supply.

Above: More advanced new feathers.

*The down feathers
are also water-proof
and provide
excellent insulation.*

The central part of the feather is called the shaft and this becomes opaque once the blood stops flowing. The shaft supports two opposite rows of barbs that together form the vane of the feather. The barbs are toothpick-like filaments arranged in a close parallel fashion on each side of the shaft. The barbs are in turn held in place by tiny barbules, essentially very small hooks. When you see a swan preening, by drawing its beak back along a feather, it is locking these barbules back into place so that the feather can work effectively again.

Because their feathers efficiently insulate the body, a swan's skin contains no sweat glands, so they have to rely on evaporative cooling from the respiratory tract. This is why you will often see birds breathing quickly or panting with their mouths open on hot days.

Other adaptations

The swan, like most other birds, has evolved some special biological adaptations which help it to fly more efficiently.

• the eyes have a transparent third eyelid called the nictitating membrane which allows the birds to blink in flight and not be blinded by the rushing air or dust particles. Swans' eyes are protected in the skull by a ring of bony plates. The distance between the lens and the retina has been increased to give better distance vision.

• the ears are entirely internal which is helpful in reducing drag through the air.

• the heart is relatively larger and more muscular than ours, giving swans a greater capacity for exercise. It is able to beat faster than ours, resulting in higher blood pressure and a more effective circulatory system.

• an air sac system, in the body cavities and some of the bones, which is connected to the lungs, allowing more efficient oxygen exchange to occur. This complex respiratory system is also helpful in maintaining body temperature.

• the beak's shape helps aerodynamically in flight, diverting the air around it and minimising drag.

• the development of a reproductive system designed with flight in mind – the young are produced outside the body (in eggs) and the reproductive organs such as the testes and ovaries only become enlarged during the breeding season – both of these features reduce weight for flight.

Flight and Navigation

Swans need plenty of space to take off and land, due to their large size. They can be seen running over the surface of the water to gain enough speed for lift-off, like an aircraft on a runway.

They fly with their neck outstretched and their feet tucked-in close to the body, to make themselves as streamlined as possible. The more aerodynamic they are, the less the drag through the air and the less energy they require to fly.

Similarly, landing needs a lot of space and mostly occurs on water, with wings, tail and feet spread out to reduce speed. Swans will fly short distances at any hour but longer journeys and migration usually take place at night. The air is cooler then, less turbulent and lower in humidity, meaning that water loss from the body is lower and flying requires less energy than it would during the heat of the day.

The mechanics of bird flight are similar to that of aircraft. Factors such as thrust, lift and drag all interact to control the way a bird flies. Thrust and lift are created by beating the wings (rather than using engines in an aircraft) and they can alter direction by changing the shape and orientation of their wings and tail (again like an aircraft). Because weight is an important factor, swans need to be careful to not eat too much and avoid becoming too heavy to get airborne.

Look carefully at a swan flying and you might be able to see them change the shape of their wings between the upstroke and the downstroke: this has the effect of minimising drag on the upstroke and maximising thrust, and thus lift, on the downstroke.

Take-off requires a lot of energy and begins with running on the water and the hard beating of the wings to generate thrust and lift.

Above: Head-on view of a Mute swan coming in to land, showing clearly the ratio of body to wing.

Right: A swan flies with its neck out-stretched and feet tucked in close to the body.

Swans can also glide for some distance without flapping their wings, especially on approach to landing. This is achieved by positioning the feathers in such a way that air cannot pass through the wings, but instead passes over the top of the wings faster than it passes underneath them; the resulting difference in air speed creates lift which allows the swan to glide. Sufficient upward lift is generated to counteract the force of gravity. A great deal of modern aviation technology has arisen from the study of birds in flight.

Above: The wing-stroke changes to glide for landing.

Swans, in common with other birds, are able to navigate over long distances, and there is much discussion about precisely how they achieve this. They probably navigate using a combination of factors, including the sun, the stars and the earth's magnetic field. It is even more remarkable when you consider that some birds travel at night and in cloudy conditions, when the sun and stars will not be visible. It is thought that birds may also be able to utilise polarised and ultraviolet light and information from their senses of sight, smell and hearing. Gravity and barometric pressure may also provide clues to help a bird navigate.

"When once you have tasted flight, you will forever walk the earth with your eyes turned skyward, for there you have been, and there you will always long to return."

– Leonardo da Vinci

Hearing and Sound

Mute swans, despite their name, are capable of making a variety of sounds. It is probably fair to say that swans do not have a 'song' as such, but the sounds they do make constitute their 'language'. The use of these sounds performs several functions, such as communication with other swans; helping with the identification and location of their young (and for the young to recognise their parents); as a warning; or as part of courtship. Swans have to be able to hear these sounds as well as produce them and so they have ears. These are located just below and behind the eyes.

Birds hear slightly differently to us. They can make and hear more subtle variations in sound than we can, such as tone and harmonic variations. They are also able to hear much shorter notes – we can hear sounds as short as 1/20 second whereas birds can discern sounds down to 1/200 second. Their range of hearing is similar to ours (which is why we can hear birdsong), although some birds such as owls have much more sensitive hearing, to help them locate their prey.

Birds can start calling very early in their lives, and sometimes even before they have hatched. Cygnets still inside the egg can

Opposite: Swans 'gape' to cool off, but they also vocalise with hisses, whistles and snorts.

56

communicate (with little whistle-like sounds) with their mother and the other cygnets to enable them all to hatch out at more or less the same time – so-called synchronised hatching.

This can be especially useful in birds like swans where the eggs are laid over a period of several days. It also allows the parents to recognise the sound of their chicks before they hatch, and vice versa. They may even be able to tell their mother if they are too hot or too cold inside the egg. Sound recognition in some

The swan's feathers exaggerate the sound of wing-beats: another form of communication.

species of birds, such as those that live in large colonies, is probably more important than sight recognition, even though their calls all sound the same to us.

Sounds are made by using the syrinx, a muscular chamber at the lower end of the windpipe (also called the trachea). Because of the swan's long neck, the windpipe is elongated and this probably works in conjunction with the syrinx in producing the swan's unique sounds. The syrinx contains several membranes, the tension and movement of which are controlled by sets of syringeal muscles located around it, thus producing various sounds. The intensity and frequency of these sounds can also be varied by changing the pressure of air flowing from the lungs to the syrinx. Birds have a larynx (in humans, the voice box) at the top end of the windpipe, but it does not contain any vocal chords.

So although the Mute swan is the least vocal of the swans, it does produce a variety of sounds, ranging from grunting, hoarse whistling and snorting (especially in communicating with their cygnets) to a loud hissing when defending their family and territory.

The Mute swan is also easily recognised by the throbbing sound of its wings during flight. This flight sound is unique to the Mute swan and is produced by its specially-shaped primary feathers which vibrate as the air passes over them. This sound is probably the mechanism by which Mute swans communicate with each other when flying – the sound travels well and can be heard up to a mile away. All the other species of swan call to each other when they are flying. In the breeding season, male swans

can sometimes be seen charging across the water, beating their wings against the surface to create a lot of noise in an aggressive territorial display – this is another form of non-vocal communication which acts as a warning. The production of sound by birds using mechanisms other than the syrinx (such as with feathers and bills) is known as sonation.

An aggressive male swan defends his territory.

A Mute swan stretching its wings after preening.

The basic structure of a Mute swan's ear is much like our own, with three chambers and an eardrum (or tympanum). The outer ear is essentially a tube from the side of the head to the eardrum. Birds lack any external, visible part of the ear like we do, although they do have a ruff of feathers around the ear opening called ear coverts. In swans this is barely visible, but it is much more so in some other birds.

Behind the eardrum is the middle ear which has a small bone stretched across it called the columella and this transmits vibrations caused by sound through to the inner ear. This contains the hearing organ – a fluid-filled chamber called the cochlea which contains hair-like cells or cilla. Movement in the cilla caused by sound vibrations creates nerve impulses which are transmitted to the brain by the auditory nerve, allowing the bird to hear.

The inner ear also contains three semi-circular canals which regulate balance and orientation, just as they do in humans. These canals contain fluid and special sensory cells that tell the bird about the position of its head relative to its surroundings.

Eyes and Sight

Vision is very important to birds and it is the most highly developed of their five senses. In fact it is the most highly developed of any animal.

The swan's eye is very similar to our eye in its basic structure and in the way it works. At the front is the lens which focuses the light on the retina (the rear wall of the eye). It is held in place by muscles and protected by the cornea at the front of the eye. The bird focuses on a subject by contracting or relaxing these muscles. The amount of light entering the eye is controlled by the iris, a thin sheet of muscle that sits in front of the lens. The opening in the iris

The fixed, deep-set eyes are compensated for by a long and flexible neck.

is called the pupil. Behind the lens is a fluid-filled chamber which forms the bulk of the eye and is filled with a jelly-like substance called the vitreous humor. The inner part of the eye is supported and protected by a tough layer of fibrous collagen which forms the 'white' of the eye. At the back is the optic nerve which carries messages from the eye to the brain.

But there are some important differences between a bird's eye and a human eye. The swan's eyes make up a much larger percentage of the weight of the head than in man, perhaps 10% for the swan compared to 1% for us. This is partly because their eyes are much wider relative to the size of the skull and partly because the swan's skull is much lighter (there is no heavy jaw bone or teeth, for a start). The benefit of having bigger eyes is that they allow much larger and sharper images to be seen.

In fact a swan's eye is actually larger than its brain. The bird's eye is also tightly fitted into its skull. This does not allow the eye to move very much, so the bird will, by necessity, have to move its head more often to see. The position of the eyes on a bird's head is closely related to its lifestyle. A swan has eyes placed further to the sides of its head than ours and this provides a greater field of vision, but it does reduce its binocular vision, the area in which both eyes can see an object.

Predatory birds such as hawks and owls have forward-facing eyes, allowing them to estimate depth of field when chasing their prey, but for a foraging bird like the swan, a wide field of vision is more important. Therefore, we can tell by the position of the swan's eyes that it feeds by foraging rather than predation.

The setting of the eyes to the side of the head is perfect for a forager, but not a hunter.

In common with other birds, swans have three eyelids. The upper and lower eyelids have very small feathers that look like eyelashes and their two eyelids are only closed when the bird rests or sleeps.

The third eyelid is called the nictitating membrane and this sits beneath the upper and lower eyelids. It has its own lubricating duct similar to our tear duct. It opens and closes horizontally across the eye, starting at the side of the eye closest to the nostril. It is this eyelid that the bird uses for blinking, crossing the eye every couple of seconds or so. Its function is to remove excess fluid and foreign matter from the eye. It may help prevent the eyes from drying out when the birds fly. It also protects the eye, for example, when bathing.

The retina (the rear wall of the eye) is densely covered with light-sensitive cells called rods and cones. The rods are sensitive to light and nocturnal birds, such as the owl, have lots of these cells in their retina. Cones work in bright light and are responsible for visual acuity (the degree of detail in an image) and for colour vision.

Birds like swans that are active mostly during the day (in other words, they are diurnal

The swan's third eyelid offers extra protection during flight and underwater.

rather than nocturnal) have far more cones than rods, and like all birds, can see in colour. Birds also tend to have a greater density of rods and cones in their retina than we do, and this gives them better long-distance vision.

Near the centre of the retina is an area called the fovea, which is where the rods and cones are at their greatest density. This means that objects directly in front appear sharper than those to the side. The lens is optically very clear and this allows it to transmit wavelengths of light down to about 350nm, which makes some ultraviolet light visible to them. Humans can only see down to about 400nm, so we cannot detect any ultraviolet light. The cones in our eyes enable us to see reds, greens and blues, and hence our vision is known as trichromatic: birds can also see these colours together with some vision in the ultraviolet part of the spectrum and so their vision is termed tetrachromatic.

It is thought that this is of benefit during courtship, when birds may be able to detect plumage patterns in UV light that are invisible to us, especially useful in birds where the sexes appear similar to the naked eye. Ultraviolet light is also used in foraging – kestrels, for example, have been shown to use this visual ability to detect urine trails on the ground left by rodents.

Birds (and reptiles too) have a structure called the pectin which protrudes from the retina into the vitreous humor and contains a rich blood supply. It is thought that this supplies nutrients and oxygen to the retina, because the bird's retina does not contain any blood vessels (unlike the human eye which has a rich supply of blood vessels).

Swans and other birds that live on water have flexible lenses in their eyes which enable them to see both above and under water. When foraging underwater, the nictitating membrane can act like a contact lens and protect the eye.

The Beak

The terms beak and bill are for the most part used interchangeably, although some scientists define the bill as the entire mouth structure and the beak as the hard keratin structure which covers the external parts of the mouth. The swan's beak (also called the rostrum) is a well-developed and obvious structure at the front of the head, which becomes a deep orange colour in adult birds. It is used for a variety of functions, in addition to feeding, such as preening, defending itself and its family, in courtship, nest building, calling and providing food for its young. It is also used to help the cygnet escape from the egg (with a specially-adapted

A Mute swan uses its flat beak, the tip of which is very sensitive, to browse the surface for food.

egg tooth, which is lost after hatching). A discoloured beak can indicate that the bird has health problems, often viral or fungal diseases.

Swans often feed by sifting through the mud and silt under-water. To help them differentiate between food and other materials, the tip of the beak contains nerve endings and is very sensitive. This sensitive area is known as the bill-tip organ and allows the swan to locate food by touch, much as we use our fingertips.

The basic structure of the beak is made of bone, parts of which are hollow and porous to reduce weight for flying. It is composed of an upper jaw, the maxilla, and a lower jaw, the mandible. It is covered with a thin horny sheath of keratin called the rhampotheca. Keratin is the same hard protein material found in our fingernails. Between the rhampotheca and the bone is a vascular layer of blood vessels and nerves.

In the Mute swan, the knob on top of the beak is part of the rhamphotheca. You can also see that the beak has two holes on its upper part, close to where it joins the head – these are the nostrils (also called nares) which connect through the hollow parts of the beak to the respiratory system. Both the tongue and the edges of the beak are serrated to help pick up small and slippery items of food. These serrations are somewhat analogous to our teeth, although they are not really used for grinding up food.

Swans can live on and feed in seawater or river estuaries, and for this purpose have developed a gland just above their eyes that allows them to drink salt water without harmful effects. This

Facing page: The keratin beak is very light and aero-dynamic for flight. Here it is being used to sift the surface water for food.

'salt gland' removes salt from the water and concentrates it into a solution that is excreted from the nostrils. This solution is cleared from the nostrils by occasionally shaking the head.

Digestion and Excretion

A bird's digestive system differs significantly from that of other animals. This is mainly because it has been designed to fulfil the bird's need to stay as light as possible for flight. Flight requires high amounts of energy and to generate this, birds eat more frequently, and digestion occurs more rapidly. A high rate of digestion also helps young birds grow quickly and adult birds to fly long distances during migration.

There are some characteristics of their digestive system that are unique to birds. The swan's serrated beak has evolved to enable it to forage and separate food from other material before it is passed down its long neck to the crop. The beak plays little part in chewing, as no saliva is produced, but food may be broken up somewhat by the process of being gathered. The crop is basically a temporary storage chamber along the oesophagus where food is kept until it is passed to the stomach. This allows hard foods such as seeds to be softened with mucus before entering the stomach.

A bird's stomach has two parts: a glandular stomach called the proventriculus and a muscular stomach, called the gizzard. The proventriculus is essentially a tube-like area which produces digestive juices such as hydrochloric acid and pepsin, and these break down the food before it is passed to the gizzard.

The gizzard, which is also known as the ventriculus, is made up of bands of muscle and contains the small stones and grit that swans periodically swallow. The combined action of the muscles and grit grind and crush the food into a fine pulp (chyme) so that any nutrients can be more easily absorbed later on. The gizzard essentially performs the same function in birds that our teeth perform for us. The only other group of animals that needed to swallow stones to help with digesting their food were the dinosaurs.

Once suitably crushed, the food is passed to the small intestine where it is digested and absorbed. The digestion process is helped by enzymes, produced by the pancreas, which break down the proteins, carbohydrates and fats. Nutrients then pass through the intestinal membranes into the bloodstream. At the end of the small intestine are several caeca, small sac-like structures which harbour bacteria which facilitate the breakdown of cellulose. The remaining food mass then passes into the large intestine, the main function of which is to absorb water and vitamins back into the bloodstream – it otherwise plays little part in the digestion process. This process is much quicker in birds than in mammals and allows faster elimination of waste to help them prepare more quickly for flight. The final holding area for waste material before it is excreted through the anus (or vent) is called the cloaca.

Waste material (or 'bird droppings') contains both solid matter and waste fluid, so birds, unlike mammals, have no need for a separate urinary system to expel excess liquid. The penis, or more accurately, the phallus, of the male swan is used solely as a copulatory organ and does not function to drain urine. Swans, ducks and geese (and a few other birds such as the ostrich) have developed this structure because they mate on water and it is needed to ensure that their sperm reaches the female.

A bathing swan.

CHAPTER FOUR

Swan Behaviour

Individual swans, just like human beings, have their own unique character and behaviour. Observing particular behaviour in one swan does not necessarily mean another will act in the same way, and this tendency towards individuality should be borne in mind when considering general behaviour in swans.

Bathing

A swan needs to keep itself clean, and this is especially important for all birds, whose feathers are complex structures which need to be kept clean to function properly.

When they want to have a wash, they fluff up their feathers to separate them, dip their heads and bodies in the water and flap their wings vigorously. This creates showers of water which pass through the feathers to clean them and can be quite dramatic and energetic. They may even roll over so that they are completely upside down in the water with their feet sticking up in the air.

They get into all sorts of awkward positions in an attempt to clean their feathers. All this movement also allows the water to clean the skin and remove unwanted guests such as mites and insects. Bathing also helps them keep cool during periods of hot dry weather.

Once finished, the bird will flap and stretch its wings and extend its neck upwards to get rid of any excess water. This bathing process can be prolonged and go on for several minutes, causing

Bathing is an energetic process which cools and cleans the swan's skin. This is followed by prolonged preening.

the bird to expend a considerable amount of energy. It is no wonder that once finished, they will usually find some shallow water or land on which to stand to preen and rest.

Sometimes birds may be seen 'sunbathing', resting on land with their wings partly outstretched. It is thought that the sun might help spread preen oil throughout the feathers or draw parasites to the surface where the bird can remove them. It may be that they just simply enjoy it too!

Occasionally, when it is dry, they may be seen rubbing their bellies on land having a 'dust bath', a process that is thought to help remove excess preen oil, particles of dry skin and insects.

Preening

Preening is a much more relaxed and delicate process than bathing. Look carefully and the swan will sometimes appear to bite its feathers. Actually it is pulling its beak along the feather to ensure that the barbs are properly aligned.

In addition, the swan has a preen (or uropygial) gland located underneath its tail. It will stretch its neck over its back, rub its beak against the gland and then spread oil that has transferred to its beak onto its feathers.

This oil is important in keeping its feathers waterproof – essential when spending such a large proportion of its life on water. It stops feathers becoming brittle and may also play a role in killing insects, lice, bacteria and fungi. Congregations of feathers on land will usually indicate a favourite preening spot.

Above: The serrated beak aligns the barbs on the feathers.

Left: Collections of feathers often indicate a favoured preening spot.

Moulting

Moulting is the process that birds go through each year to replace their worn feathers with new ones. This takes a lot of energy, so it usually happens when egg laying has finished and food is plentiful. It is a prolonged process and takes about six weeks for a swan to replace all its feathers. During this time, the swans are unable to fly (unlike most birds that moult a bit at a time so they are never unable to fly). In a breeding pair of swans, they moult at separate times, the female first, so that one of the pair can protect the other and their young.

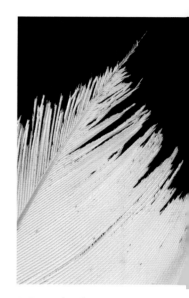

Worn feathers are removed in the moulting process.

Resting and Sleeping

Swans need sleep just as we do, but they do not sleep for long periods. All birds tend to sleep (or roost) frequently but for short periods of time (sometimes only seconds) and it is the same for swans.

They can often be seen, particularly during the middle of the day, sitting on the ground or floating on the water with their head tucked back under a wing. Sometimes they will go to sleep standing on one leg, with the other tucked up tightly against their body, behaviour which allows them to conserve their body heat by minimising contact with the ground. If they stood on both legs, there would be twice as much skin in contact with the ground and twice as much heat loss. Watch a resting swan and you will see it frequently open and close one of its eyes. This is a behavioural technique called 'uni-hemispheric sleep', in which one half of the brain is awake and the other is asleep. This allows it to get some sleep whilst still maintaining awareness of its surroundings and, in particular, of any potential predators.

Swans are largely diurnal (active during the day) and therefore sleep mostly at night, but they have been known to adapt their routine to whatever is the safest. So, for example, if they are harassed by people during the day they will become more active at night. Swans have preferred roosting sites where they feel more secure, and they can often be seen flying off to those places as dusk approaches. Sometimes swans swim with one foot out of the water – this is not because there is something wrong with it: it is another mechanism used to regulate its temperature and to conserve energy. It is able to lose or absorb heat from the sun through its feet.

A sleeping swan.

Breeding

The Mute swan is the only swan that breeds naturally in the UK and is our only resident swan. They may choose a mate once they attain their adult all-white plumage, but will generally not start breeding until they are three or four years old, sometimes later, and some may even remain single throughout their lives. They are renowned for staying with the same mate for life (in other words, they are monogamous), but whilst this is generally true, it is not always the case.

Life is about raising young as well as surviving, and hence continued failure to produce offspring may stimulate a bird to look elsewhere for a new mate. Breeding failure may be due to a variety of reasons, such as building the nest in an inappropriate place (where it might be more vulnerable to predators or flooding), or just the inexperience of the birds. Older, more experienced pairs, tend to be more successful in rearing their young.

Swans are creatures of habit and will generally live and nest in the same place year after year. Once swans have paired up and identified a suitable place to live, they become fiercely territorial and will defend their patch of water from other swans and larger water birds such as geese, with tremendous vigour. This is why you only see one pair of swans on a small lake or stretch of river, but on larger bodies of water where there is an abundance of food and space, there can be several pairs. Although swans are territorial, they can exist and breed in colonies, such as that at Abbotsbury Swannery in Dorset where there are over 100 breeding pairs

in close proximity to each other in the breeding season. This situation has been influenced by past domestication and the continued provision of food and so is not entirely natural, although the birds are free to come and go as they choose. When groups of swans are seen, they tend to be immature or non-breeding birds, which can be quite sociable, especially if food is regularly provided for them or easily available.

Previous page: Swans are fiercely territorial and defend their patch with a great show of aggression.

Defending territory and protecting young is one of the tasks of the male swan during the breeding season. If an intruder gets too close, the male will charge across the water towards the offending bird in an attempt to drive it away (see previous page). Usually this is successful, but on occasion may result in fierce prolonged conflict and even death for one of the birds. To enable them to use their wings most effectively for defending themselves, they have developed an enlarged carpal bone halfway along the wing (at a point equivalent to where our wrist is) with which the birds can inflict a painful, serious blow by beating their wings. Their necks are strong enough to hold other birds and small animals under-water, gripping with their beaks, in order to drown them. A male may even drown cygnets belonging to another family that stray into his territory.

Below: Swans can fight, even to the death, using the enlarged carpal bone on their wings as an offensive weapon.

Swans frequently exhibit a behaviour known as 'busking' where the neck is curved backwards over the body, the wings half-raised and the bird swims forcefully through the water. This aggressive threat

Above: Busking, an aggressive, warning, territorial display.

display is intended to scare off unwanted visitors to the swan's territory, including people, and is mainly shown by the males, but also by the females to a lesser extent.

The swan is a large bird, and this has consequences in terms of its breeding. It cannot breed more than once in a season, unlike many other water-birds that raise more than one family each year. This is because the young take a long time to reach an age where they are able to look after themselves, and the defence of territory over this period of time takes a lot of energy from the adults. This, together with the fact that both parents look after the young, means that, in evolutionary terms, a monogamous relationship is the best strategy for breeding.

*Territorial disputes
can lead to injury or
drowning although
this is rare.*

Courtship and Mating

On the water in early spring, an elaborate courtship begins. The pair will swim around closely together for several days, the male often following the moves of the female. They will eventually then face each other and turn and bob their heads together, often entwining their necks and dipping their heads and beaks into the water. In younger birds, courtship and sexual activity is limited to this mutual head-turning, often with the birds fluffing-up their neck feathers. They can be seen to 'kiss' beaks and form the traditional heart shape with their necks. In older, more experienced pairs, this phase of head-turning and dipping their heads into the water can be quite prolonged, especially in the build-up to mating.

Once this occurs in unison, the male will then climb on top of the female, biting the back of her neck to help him stay there. At times she becomes completely submerged, sometimes with even her head underwater. It can appear as if the male is trying to drown her. They will both slightly spread their wings to help them maintain this position. Copulation (mating) itself is fairly brief, and afterwards they rise out of the water together with their necks entwined once again. Synchronised head-turning is often performed again at this stage, accompanied by a few snorting noises. It is a beautiful spectacle to witness.

The swans then swim away from each other and begin to wash themselves by vigorously splashing around for several minutes, before finding a quiet spot in which to preen. Mating usually takes place in the few weeks prior to egg-laying, but can take place at other times (and more frequently than is required to fertilise the eggs) and this may be important in maintaining the pair bond. Occasional mating with other swans outside the pair has also been observed, although this does not appear to adversely affect the pair bond. In fact swans can be just as fickle as humans in their relationships with each other: if the opportunity arises, they can 'cheat' on their partners, and some males have been observed raising two families at the same time.

Swans usually only breed when they are three or four years old and at that point they tend to pair for life.

This courting and mating sequence runs from top left, clockwise, on each page.

Stages include, mirroring, entwining, submerging, mounting and post-coital preening

*Mirroring
one another's
movements, before
and after mating,
is an important part
of courtship and
bonding.*

Nesting, Egg Laying and Incubation

A swan's nest is a very large affair, sometimes more than two metres in diameter, and could perhaps be more accurately described as a 'heap of vegetation' rather than a nest. It takes several weeks to build and is shaped in the middle by the swan's weight. Usually built at the water's edge or on a small island, it is made from vegetation and sticks found in and around the water. The nest is mainly constructed by the male – once complete he will invite the female to inspect it and she will begin to lay her eggs in it if she finds it acceptable. Sometimes, however, she may refuse and force him to build another nest in a different location. Several nests may be built before she finds one to her liking. The female may add to the nest with material brought to her by her mate. Once a suitable and successful site has been agreed upon, the pair will often use the same nest year after year.

Egg-laying usually begins in April, but can be as early as mid-March if there has been a mild winter. The average number of eggs in a clutch is about six, but up to 13 can be laid. Older, more

Above: The female will only lay in a nest that is to her liking.

Right: Incubation only begins after all the eggs have been laid, which can take over two weeks.

experienced birds, generally lay fewer eggs. The eggs are a chalky greenish-grey colour and weigh about 350 grams, among the largest bird's eggs in the world. Eggs are laid every 1-2 days and the female will only begin sitting on the nest and incubating them once she has finished laying.

She will stay on the nest almost continuously, usually for about 35 days, until they all hatch, only occasionally leaving it for brief periods to feed. When she does, the male will guard the nest or even sit on the eggs himself to protect them whilst she is away. For this reason, the pen (female) will eat a lot of food before nesting and then lose a lot of weight during incubation. If the pair loses these eggs, for example to a predator such as a fox, a second clutch may be laid.

Below: A nest by the water's edge, or on an island, is the favoured spot.

Once the eggs are laid, they must be kept warm if they are to develop, and swans use their body heat to incubate their eggs. Towards the end of the egg-laying period, the female develops a brood patch, an area of her breast which loses its feathers and develops more blood vessels to bring warm blood to the surface of the skin. The brood patch allows the pen's body heat to be more efficiently used in providing a constant warm environment for the eggs: essential since feathers are poor conductors of heat (as we know, they are actually very good at insulation).

97

When a swan returns to the nest to resume incubation, it can be seen to go through characteristic 'settling' movements in order to bring the brood patch into contact with the eggs. The feathers on the breast soon re-grow once the eggs have hatched, restoring the pen's ability to keep this area warm and dry again.

She will periodically turn the eggs with her beak to ensure that they are evenly incubated.

A pen moves the eggs around to fit against her warm 'brood patch', and she will turn them to maintain an even temperature.

98

Hatching, cygnets and growing–up

All the eggs normally hatch within a 24-hour period. As the eggs have relatively thick shells, it can be quite a struggle for the cygnet to break free – it can sometimes take up to 48 hours to complete the exit, from when it first breaks through the shell. To help them, the cygnets have a hard tip to their bill, called the 'egg tooth', which is used to break through the shell.

Cygnets are nidifugous – this means that, unlike most birds, they are born with their eyes open; they are covered in down; and are able to leave the nest very soon after hatching. However, newborn cygnets remain together in the nest until all the eggs have hatched.

Hatching often involves a long struggle to emerge.

Once they are all hatched, both parents will encourage them to the water by making various grunting sounds. The newborn cygnets are covered in light grey down feathers which are water-

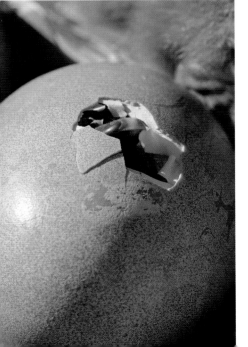

proof, allowing them to swim straight away. They weigh about 170 grams when they hatch. The parents are very vigilant at this stage, staying very close to them at all times.

When on water, the cygnets stay close together, typically swimming directly behind their mother, with the father often bringing up the rear. During their first few days of life, the whole family will often return to the nest at night for added protection, where the female will keep them warm under her wings, because baby swans can be susceptible to hypothermia. The more dedicated the parents are during these early days, the greater the chances are that their offspring will survive. Sometimes inexperienced birds may appear unsure of what to do, or unaware of where some of their cygnets are, resulting in unfortunate chicks being trampled to death in and around the nest.

Sometimes the parents kill or abandon a cygnet for no apparent reason, but undoubtedly this is because

A mere 170 grams, but they can swim almost as soon as they hatch.

If the mother leaves the nest temporarily, to feed, the male takes over.

they are aware of some deformity or abnormality in the cygnet that is not obvious to us. Cygnets can also be lost to a variety of predators like fox, mink, crows, herons, turtles and large predatory fish such as pike, so the parents must be ever-vigilant.

Swans are dedicated parents, and, during the first few days after hatching, when they are at their most vulnerable, the parents will allow the cygnets to shelter or hitch a ride on their backs *(see overleaf)*. It can be very amusing watching them struggling to climb up onto their mother's back, often tumbling upside down back into the water, or pushing and shoving each other to get the 'best' position.

The parents will also shelter the chicks under their wings on land, to protect them from predators and from becoming too hot or cold.

If one of the parents should die or disappear, the surviving swan remains dedicated to the family and will take over and rear the young on its own.

The archetypal 'ugly duckling'.

With a plentiful supply of food, the young cygnets are able to grow at a surprising rate and can be almost adult size by October. It is during this period that the cygnets take on their least attractive appearance, and with their stubby little developing wings they really do look like the 'ugly duckling' of Hans Christian Andersen fame. Their grey down is gradually replaced by brown and then white feathers, giving juvenile birds a mottled, almost dirty appearance.

They stay together with their parents as a family unit until the spring, when the urge to breed once again takes over the adult birds and the young are, quite literally, chased away. This can be

Juvenile swans with parent, where they will stay until about a year old.

A parent chases away a juvenile swan from the family group.

quite aggressive, especially if the youngsters are reluctant to leave, and can sometimes result in them being killed by their parents if they refuse to go.

Once they leave their parents, young swans usually join up with other adolescent birds until they become old enough to find a mate and breed themselves. Most groups of swans seen on rivers and lakes comprise such birds, together with non-breeding adults. It is not until they moult for the first time the following summer that they develop their all-white adult plumage, although their beaks remain grey (or 'blue') for another year. Adult birds are recognised by their all-white plumage and orange beak – the darker the beak, the older the individual. The knob on top of the beak also becomes more pronounced with age.

Feeding

Swans tend to spend the majority of their time on water, so naturally that is where they find most of their food. Their diet consists mainly of aquatic vegetation, and a healthy bird can consume up to four kilos of it in a day. Their long necks have evolved to allow them to eat plants on both the riverbank and bottom-growing vegetation such as Eel Grass, Tasselweed and pondweeds such as Potamogeton and Myriophyllum.

They do not usually dive for their food like some other aquatic birds, but instead 'dabble' – dipping and splashing their beaks in the water. Rarely, they have been known to dive, but this only occurs when food is difficult to obtain, or as a last resort when faced with danger.

Swans will also eat a wide variety of aquatic animals, including small fish, frogs, tadpoles, worms, small crustaceans and various insects, making them omnivorous. Their heads and necks sometimes show brownish colouration, the result of mineral staining from foraging amongst the silt in the riverbed. You can often see them upended with their tails in the air foraging

Right: A swan can consume 4 kilos of weed daily.

Below: Dabbling for food.

Overleaf: a mother teaches her cygnets to forage in a food-rich backwater.

107

underwater. Sometimes they can be seen with their heads and necks extended along the surface of the water, looking for surface food.

They can also be seen 'treading water', where they use their feet to paddle against the current, staying in the same place, deliberately disturbing insects and vegetation in the water, especially for their cygnets (*see previous page*). On the coast they have been known to feed on molluscs, while inland, they can often be seen congregating in small groups to feed on crops such as watercress, corn and other cereals.

Swans, like many birds, will also eat bread and people often feed them regularly at local lakes and rivers. Many have become habituated to people and can be fed from the hand, although any bread should ideally be seeded and thrown into the water.

With their long necks, swans only need to up-end like this in deeper water.

In some places with high concentrations of swans, severe damage can be done to underwater vegetation, sometimes affecting other aquatic life and even the flow of water. When this is excessive, it can become necessary to cull numbers of swans in certain locations.

Vocalisation and communication

The Mute swan is probably so-called because in general it is much less vocal than other swans such as Whooper and Bewick's swans, and because it does not call when flying. But they do make a variety of grunting and snorting noises, especially when communicating with their cygnets, sometimes in combination with head raising or fluffing-out their feathers. They will also make a loud hissing sound when people or predators get too close, in the protection of their young or when other birds (such as other swans or geese) enter their territory – in Russia it has been called the 'hissing swan' for this reason.

Parents communicate with their cygnets with a variety of grunts and snorts.

The sound with which the feathers of the Mute swan resonate can carry over a mile.

Those who work regularly with Mute swans think that they may be able to make as many as eight different types of sound, each likely to have its own specific meaning. Cygnets make a characteristic high-pitched piping sound when communicating with their parents.

Although Mute swans do not call in flight, the movement of air through their feathers when flying does create a unique 'whining' sound. It is thought that this sound can travel up to a mile or more, suggesting that it might be of use in communicating with other swans in flight.

CHAPTER FIVE

Enemies of the Swan

L ike all wildlife, swans sometimes suffer hardship and harm from natural causes. Significant variations in the weather can have a major impact. Very cold weather and freezing conditions can make it difficult for the birds to access water (because of ice) and find food, making them weaker and more susceptible to pneumonia and other respiratory infections. Some birds even become trapped in the ice in particularly severe conditions.

Excessively warm and dry conditions can cause heat stress and dehydration. Heavy rainfall, especially in the breeding season, can be very harmful to young cygnets which have difficulty keeping warm and dry, and flooding can wash away nests and eggs.

In many areas, aquatic vegetation is becoming scarce and the increase in riverside construction and sheer numbers of moored boats can make it very difficult for swans to access the riverbank

117

to feed, so many stretches of river are now becoming difficult places for swans to live and breed.

Although swans have few regular predators, many are lost each year to opportunistic predation. Foxes are probably responsible for killing the highest number of swans, mainly taking injured birds or those that choose to roost in accessible places.

The top wild predator of the swan is the fox.

118

Large fish such as pike and perch have been seen taking young cygnets from the water surface. In fact, most carnivorous predatory animals will take a cygnet if the opportunity presents itself, although this is not part of their normal diet. Large predatory birds like ravens and gulls will also take unguarded cygnets, and, exceptionally, eagles have even been known to attack fully-grown swans in flight.

But one non-native predator in particular has had a significant negative effect on the numbers of swans – the mink. This animal is a member of the Mustelid family, similar to a ferret, and is an introduced species in Britain. It was brought here from North America in the late 1920s and bred for its fur. There have been many escapees and they are now successfully established in the wild. In some areas, such as along the River Thames, many swan

Unguarded cygnets can be the prey of the raven.

fatalities are the result of mink attacks – they have a reputation for being very aggressive and are known to kill animals and birds even when they are not hungry. Unfortunately, mink numbers are on the increase and they have no hesitation in attacking an adult swan. Even if they fail to kill the bird, the resultant injuries are often severe enough to lead to a slow and painful death. Young cygnets in particular are very vulnerable to attack.

Fighting amongst swans can also result in some fatalities, either because of males fiercely defending their territories against each other or by killing another pair's cygnets because they have come too close to their own. Adolescent birds can be driven away from their parents' territory when they are old enough to fly, and occasionally reluctant birds are killed if they refuse to go.

Increasing numbers of Canada geese, which seem to breed very readily, can also make life difficult for swans. A swan can easily chase away a single pair of Canada geese on its territory, but the presence of greater numbers may cause the swans to not breed or to be forced into finding another area in which to live.

There are, of course, a variety of natural diseases that also affect our swans. Some of the more common ailments are:

A mink will attack even an adult swan, often resulting in a slow death due to injury.

The massive influx of Canada geese can cause the swan to move territory or refuse to breed.

• Botulism – swans often feed from the riverbed and so can pick up certain anaerobic bacteria that produce a neurotoxin called botulinum. This affects the bird's muscles which control swallowing and breathing, and one of the first symptoms is an inability of the swan to hold up its head and neck properly. The condition is usually fatal in birds left in the wild but can be treated in captivity. Botulism is more prevalent in unusually hot and dry conditions.

• Clostridium infection – in the right environmental conditions, clostridium bacteria can take hold and decimate populations.

• Bumblefoot – a general swelling or fibrous callus on the foot, sometimes with bacterial infection. More often associated with captive swans, it has also been found in wild birds. This condition may also be seen after birds have crash-landed on hard unnatural surfaces such as tarmac.

• Bird or Avian flu – this is a general term for illness caused by a variety of strains of the influenza virus. Several strains of bird flu occur naturally in populations of wild birds and usually only

cause mild symptoms. When infection does take hold, there can be a wide variety of symptoms such as difficulty in standing, walking and flying (a general lack of co-ordination), discolouration and lethargic behaviour. The virus is carried in the intestines and transmitted through contact with the birds' droppings and by sharing sources of drinking water. Bird flu can be prevalent in swans, and migrating birds have been found to significantly spread the flu virus around the world during epidemics. Some strains of bird flu can pass across the species barrier to humans.

● various other viral infections, such as duck virus enteritis and necrotic enteritis. In 2011, after the particularly severe preceding winter, nearly 200 swans were found dead or dying on the River Thames, most of these attributed to viral infection.

● Aspergillosis – this is a fungal infection of the respiratory system and is relatively common in water birds. It is caused by the spores of the Aspergillus fungus which is found almost everywhere in the environment. Usually the fungus does not cause disease but weak or stressed birds are susceptible to infection. Symptoms include difficulty in breathing and loss of appetite and if untreated can result in death.

● Pink discoloration – some birds' feathers turn pink in colour prior to or during the moult. This discoloration is caused by bacterial infection but fortunately it is easily removed with washing-up liquid.

● Parasites – swans are subject to a variety of parasites such as worms (nematodes, gizzard worms, heart worms, tape worms etc), various lice and protozoa.

Left: A territorial dispute.

Right: A dead swan in the Outer Hebrides.

CHAPTER SIX

Swan Domestication

There is of course a more prosaic reason why the swan has been so important to Man throughout history: as food. There are many records suggesting that humans have harvested all kinds of waterfowl, swans included, for centuries, and archaeological evidence indicates that swans have been eaten since prehistoric times. Hunting for swans was a common pastime for the Romans, mostly for gathering food but also for leisure.

The Bible (in both Leviticus and Deuteronomy) is however rather negative towards the swan, classifying it as 'unclean' and a bird that 'ye shall not eat'. This may have arisen as a result of an incorrect translation from the Hebrew word 'tinshemeth'. Some versions of the Bible have translated this word into 'ibis' rather than 'swan', and this is more likely to be correct, as there is no particular reason to consider the latter an unclean animal.

It is not surprising that swans were a source of food for our ancestors. The birds were easy to find and catch; especially during the moult when they are unable to fly, and before the young birds are old enough to fly. From early times swans were kept in a semi-domesticated state as a source of food. Sometimes cygnets would be caught from the wild and kept in 'swanneries' within the grounds of monasteries or castles where they were allowed to breed. Today the only remaining managed colony of nesting Mute swans in the world is at Abbotsbury in Dorset, England, where there are over a thousand birds. The Swannery was established in the 11th century by Benedictine Monks who farmed the swans for their lavish banquets, but of course the birds are now no longer kept for food and have instead become a major tourist attraction.

Left: The last remaining private 'swannery' of nesting Mute swans is in Dorset, and owned by the Ilchester family.

Historically, the reigning Monarch was entitled to claim ownership (so-called Royal Prerogative) of any unmarked Mute swans swimming in open water, or to give such rights to others. It is not known when this custom began but the first written record of the swan as a royal bird dates back to the 12th century and relates to a number of birds in a captive state, suggesting that the custom of owning swans may have already been in existence for several years.

Because of their value as food, swans became prized commodities and were regularly traded between noblemen. Historical records show that the swan was the most expensive eating bird to

The Mute swan: a royal bird since the 12th century.

purchase – for example, its price in 1274 was set at three shillings compared to four pence for a pheasant and five pence for a goose – so it was the most profitable bird to raise. In 1482, a statute of King Edward IV, commonly referred to as the Act of Swans, limited the ownership of swans to wealthy landowners, provided that they marked their swans to show ownership and kept them on their own land (by clipping their wings so that they could not fly away). If a swan wandered beyond the owner's land, they had a year and a day to find it and bring it back to their property. Ownership of swans thus became a symbol of status in society. The relative cost of rearing swans for most people was small as they were left to forage naturally on the owners' land and only supplied with additional grain during the winter months, a state of semi-domestication which is generally how the swans were kept. They were also raised so that they could be given as gifts by the Monarchy or wealthy landowners to deserving individuals or organisations.

Each year the swans were rounded up during an annual census, 'Swan Upping', which was under the control of the Crown. This took place in late July when the adult birds were in moult and

The swan count was done in late July, during the moult, when the swans cannot fly.

the young swans too small to fly. The cygnets were given the mark of the parent bird: if the parents belonged to two different owners, the brood was shared between them. When there was an odd number of cygnets, the owner of the male bird was given the extra cygnet. Some cygnets were released to maintain a breeding stock and anyone caught stealing birds was severely punished. Today, Swan Upping continues by tradition, but only in a limited form.

Because many landowners kept swans, some mechanism to indicate ownership was needed, especially where birds were kept and fed communally. It was also necessary to identify birds

129

that had strayed or been stolen. Most families already had their own mark, which was placed over the house, on cattle, horses and other livestock, and it was a logical progression to use this same mark on their swans.

There were four main options for marking a bird to show which family it belonged to.

• The most common method was to indent the upper part of the beak with a combination of circular and triangular shapes and lines, usually made by cutting with a sharp knife.

• The second way was to similarly mark the lower mandible. Some marks were very elaborate and it seems unlikely that a knife would have been adequate – possibly a thin hot iron rod was used for these, in a type of 'branding' process.

• The legs and feet were sometimes marked with notches or holes cut into the webbing of the foot, or a claw was removed.

• Pinioning one of the wings was the final way of marking a bird, the side of the bird being used in conjunction with its other marks to indicate ownership.

These marks themselves became valuable commodities and the rights to the patterning were often traded for considerable sums of money. The details of all of these marks were officially recorded in registers, frequently a roll of parchment, and hence these became known as 'swan rolls'.

Left: A drawing of a swan's beak recreating some of the traditional identification markings of the private owners.

Other mechanisms may also have been used, such as that depicted on a manuscript in the Bodleian Library in Oxford dating back to 1340: this shows a bird confined to a square pen with its neck being held while someone makes a hole in its foot with a hammer and punch.

These identifying marks were registered with the Crown under the supervision of the Royal Swanmaster and all unmarked birds were considered the property of the Monarch. Hence the swan became known as a 'Royal Bird'.

On the River Thames, the *Act of Swans* also allowed both the Livery Companies of the City of London, the Company of Vintners and the Company of Dyers, to own swans on open water on the river provided that they were clearly marked: a single nick on the bill indicated ownership by the Dyers and two nicks for the Vintners' swans. The original right of these Companies to own swans is thought to have existed from as far back as the 12th century, and because it was never legally challenged, they have retained that right, as the law says, 'by prescription'.

During the 16th century, the turkey was introduced into England from the United States of America. The turkey was easier to rear and tasted better than swan and gradually replaced it as the poultry of choice at banquets and feasts. This introduction, and the semi-domestication of swans in swanneries, probably helped save the wild swan from extinction in the UK.

The turkey put the swan off the menu. It tasted much better.

131

As swans became less valuable, the importance of Swan Upping began to diminish and by the mid-nineteenth century few people retained their right to own swans. However, the tradition of Swan Upping has persisted although the emphasis is now on conservation rather than food and ownership. Apart from the Crown, only three bodies have maintained their right to own swans: the Ilchester family (which owns the swans at Abbotsbury Swannery); and the two Livery Companies, The Dyers and The Vintners. Today these two Companies together with the Crown maintain the tradition of Swan Upping on the River Thames and this still occurs each year in July.

Eating Swan

Swan was usually roasted in the same way as other large game birds such as goose. Recipes for cooking the birds were somewhat vague: quantities of ingredients used were fairly arbitrary and cooking temperatures and times were not provided as it was difficult to accurately measure and control oven temperature. Swan meat was supposed to be quite tasty, if a little tough. It has been described as being like 'fishy mutton' and hard to digest. Cygnets of about six months old were considered to be the most tender and tasty, while older birds would be more frequently used in stews and hashes.

From ancient times, roast swan was typical fare on banquet menus for Royalty and the rich. Historical records suggest that up to fifty swans might have been included on the menu of an important feast. It was often made the centrepiece of a banquet, sometimes being re-dressed in its skin and feathers so that it appeared as it did before being cooked, with the neck and wings being held in place by skewers. The entrails, such as the gizzard, liver and blood, were also used to make a kind of sauce called

chawdron or chaudouw. Occasionally the neck was cut off and served separately as 'pudding de swan neck'. Swan meat was also used in the making of various pies, particularly when mixed with other meats. The eggs were also eaten, and used in making drinks, as well as a baking ingredient. Although swan was often the food of choice at significant feasts, it was not really consumed on a daily basis and so was not considered a staple food.

Above: A stuffed swan adorns the banqueting plate at a formal dinner for the Vintners' Livery Company.

It appears that swan (or cygnet) last appeared on menus at the end of the 19th century. Nowadays, of course, swan is not eaten, as it is a protected bird, but the tradition of its association with food has continued.

It is common for food such as pastries, cakes and ice cream to be served in the shape of a swan. Some traditional annual feasts, such as The Vintners' Company Annual Swan Feast in London, still often serve so-called 'mock swan' or 'cygnet' – usually turkey stuffed and formed into the shape of a swan (the swan presented on the platter is stuffed with straw). The neck and wings (made of wax) are added, with the beak, nostrils and eyes painted on to complete the illusion.

Use of Swan Feathers, Bones and Feet

Swan feathers have been put to various uses throughout history, one of the most visible being that of a writing instrument, or quill pen. It was the principal writing instrument for over a thousand years until the 19th century, when the metal pen was patented in America and took over as the writing instrument of choice.

The quill pen first came into use in the 6th century and superseded the use of the reed, favoured, for example, by the ancient Egyptians for writing on papyrus. The word 'pen' comes from the Latin word 'penna' which means feather. Goose feathers were most commonly used but those from the swan were considered the best and most expensive. A quill made from a swan's feather was said to out-last 50 goose quills, although some people preferred to use goose as they found the swan's quills too stiff for writing. Depending on the thickness and quality of the line required by the writer, feathers of other birds such as the crow and owl were also used. The strongest quills came from the primary flight feathers – these being named by the order in which the feathers are fixed in the wing. The first is called the pinion (derived from the Latin 'pinna' meaning wing) and is the one most favoured by writers (hence the term 'pinioning' – removing part of the wing from which the flight feathers grow so that the bird cannot fly). The second and third primary flight feathers were also used but the other feathers were considered unsatisfactory for writing purposes. Feathers from the left wing were said to be favoured because they curved outward and away when used by a right-handed scribe.

The swan quill pen was superior to that of the goose, and replaced the reed in the 6th century.

After a feather had been plucked or selected, the shaft needed to be carved to the correct shape. For this, a sharp knife was needed – this became known as the 'penknife' (i.e. feather knife). Because each quill was hand-produced, no two quills were the same and it became a skilled art to select, clean and carve each writing quill. The barbs of the feather were always removed because they were considered an impractical distraction. The fancy fully plumed quill is for the most part a theatrical embellishment with little basis in reality.

The use of quills went into decline in the 19th century after the invention of the metal pen and the first practical fountain pen was patented by Lewis Waterman in 1884.

Swan feathers were also used for making arrows. Although arrow-making is now predominantly a pastime, it was once an essential survival skill, with a strong and durable arrow one of the basic hunting tools. Feathers from the swan and goose were often used, as they were large, strong and naturally waterproof.

Because of their superb insulating qualities, down feathers from swans were popular in making duvets and pillows. Swan feathers may also have been used decoratively in hat-making. At the Vintners' Hall in London there is a beautiful cape made from swans' down feathers.

Swans were sacred birds for many groups of people around the world, who would often use swan feathers as part of their ceremonial dress or costume: for example, the ancient Celtic bards (poets) used swan feathers and skin to make the Tugen, the ceremonial Bardic Cloak, and American Indians also used swan feathers as part of their substantial head-dresses.

The swan's feathers had a number of important uses: as fletches (arrow fins) in archery, as quill pens for writers, and the down was always superb for bedding.

136

Historically, when animals were killed for food, it was common practice to make use of the parts which were not eaten, and this was true of swans too. The bones, particularly those from the leg, were used to make whistles and flutes and the soft leathery feet were made into purses and tobacco pouches.

CHAPTER SEVEN

Swan Upping

The annual census of Mute swans, traditionally known as Swan Upping, has taken place since the 12th century and still occurs today, albeit only in ceremonial form. It still takes place during the third week of July, for the same historical reasons, but is now confined to certain stretches of the River Thames and its tributaries in Middlesex, Surrey, Buckinghamshire, Berkshire and Oxfordshire. The swans are counted, but of course no longer eaten.

The term 'Swan Upping' probably derives from the practice of lifting the birds out of the water to catch them for marking, and to see whether or not their feet were already marked. So to 'up a swan' meant to catch one and lift it out of the water.

The two Livery Companies, The Vintners and The Dyers, together with The Crown, have continued the tradition of Swan Upping.

The Swan Upping ceremony today begins at Sunbury and ends at Abingdon, a distance of 79 miles, and takes place over five days. The Queen's Swan Marker together with The Queen's Swan Warden (a Professor of Ornithology at the University of Oxford) and the 'Swan Uppers' from the Crown and the two livery companies row up the Thames in six traditional wooden skiffs.

The Queen's Swan Uppers wear traditional scarlet uniforms and each boat flies the appropriate flags and pennants. The Queen's Swan Marker's duty is to count and allocate ownership of the cygnets, and ensure that the population of swans is maintained.

Above: Swan Uppers preparing for the day's activities on the Thames at Marlow.

Right: The Swan Upping banner of the Vintners' Boat.

Overleaf: First catch your swan! Easier during the moult when they can't fly.

When a family of swans is sighted, a cry of 'All Up' is given and the boats converge on the swans, catch them and take them ashore for examination and marking. The birds are checked for general health and any signs of injury, such as entanglement with fishing wire. Some injuries can be dealt with on the riverbank, but with more severe injuries (such as swallowing a fishing hook), the birds may have to be taken to a rescue centre for treatment and recuperation. Cygnets are weighed and measured to obtain estimates of growth-rates before being released. School children are encouraged to witness the catching and examination of the birds at close quarters. Thus the focus of the ceremony these days is very much on welfare, conservation and education.

The young birds are also marked according to tradition, but with rings rather than nicks in their beaks; one ring for the Dyers' birds and two (one on each leg) for the Vintners' birds. Those swans belonging to the Crown are still left unmarked. The birds are then returned to the water, ensuring that the cygnets are not separated from their parents.

On passing Windsor castle, the rowers stand to attention in their boats with oars raised and salute 'Her Majesty The Queen, Seigneur of the Swans'. In 2009, The Queen attended the ceremony for the first time in her reign, this being the only time a monarch has witnessed the event in centuries.

The Swan Upping record provides important information about the number of swans on the river over the course of time, and is a useful indicator of the

general health of the river. Numbers of swans were low at the beginning of the last century, but rose steadily until the mid 1960s, when numbers declined dramatically as a result of lead poisoning.

A maximum number of 76 pairs of swans with cygnets was recorded in the past, and this had reduced to only seven in 1985. Swan numbers

The Queen's Swan Uppers wear scarlet uniforms and travel in a traditional wooden skiff.

Left: A banner of the Thames Vintage Boat Club.

are slowly increasing, but there are still far fewer than have been recorded in the past.

Manoeuvring the boats – and the birds – towards the bank: the capturing process in Swan Upping.

The Queen's Swan Marker also provides information and advice to various organisations throughout the country on swan welfare and conservation. He monitors the health of local swan populations and helps with the rescue of sick and injured birds, working closely with swan rescue centres.

CHAPTER EIGHT

Language & the Swan

The word 'swan' has been used for many hundreds of years and not surprisingly has been incorporated into our language in various ways. It has descended unchanged from the old Saxon word 'swan' or 'suan'. Prior to that it is likely that these and similar words from other languages (such as 'svan' or 'schwan') were derived from the early Indo-European word 'swen' or 'swon' which means to make a sound or to sing. This suggests that the swan may have originally received its name from the sound it was thought to make, but this is a little surprising since the Mute swan makes little vocal noise. However, perhaps the name is a connection to the ancient belief that swans sing only once, just before their death, or possibly refers to the sound made by air passing through the feathers in the wings when they fly.

The dictionary defines the noun 'swan' as 'any large aquatic bird of the genera Cygnus and Coscoroba, having a long neck and usually a white plumage'. This is the commonest and most used definition. However, other uses of the word, and adaptations of it, have found their way into our language over the course of time. These have been mostly derived from the behaviour and appearance of the bird although they are for the most part rarely used nowadays. Examples include:

- **Swan dive**: North American term for a shallow dive.

- **Swanling**: another word for cygnet (analogous to the words duckling and gosling).

- **Swan neck**: a tube or a rail etc curved like a swan's neck.

- **Swanskin**: a type of brushed flannel cotton twill fabric.

- **Swannie**: an all-weather heavy woollen shirt.

- **Swan song**: the last work or performance, for example of a musician before retirement, originating from the ancient Greek belief that the swan was silent except for the one song it sang when dying, a notion seized on by western poets and artists.

- **'Swan'** has also been used as an epithet or title to describe a sweet singer or poet particularly noted for their graceful verse, such as William Shakespeare, who was sometimes known as the 'Swan of Avon'.

Below: a swan dive.

Bottom: swanning around aimlessly.

Above: serene and majestic in motion.

As a verb, **'to swan'** is rarely used, but it does have three meanings:

- **to swan around**: to move around aimlessly, without any real intention or destination, also 'swanning around'.

- **to move like a swan**, majestically or effortlessly.

- **to swan**: to exclaim in surprise or curse (used mainly in the southern United States).

We also have these terms, mainly relating to the semi-domestication of swans:

- **Swanherd**: a person who looks after (and herds) swans

- **Swan pit**: an artificial enclosed pool in which swans were kept for fattening

- **Swannage**: the payment made for the privilege of keeping swans

- **Swan roll**: a book or roll in which were recorded the names of owners and their swan marks in a particular area

- **Swannery**: a place where swans were kept and bred

- **Swan Upping**: the practice of catching and marking swans every year

- **Swan mark**: various designs cut or branded onto the beak or foot to indicate swan ownership

In addition, some words were also introduced to describe particular aspects of swan-keeping, and as the practice disappeared, so too did the use of the words:

- **Airie** – the nest or nest site

- **Barans** – swans in their third year that were not yet breeding

- **Brood swans** – adult birds paired for nesting

- **Butted** – a pinioned bird

- **Blue-bill** – a young swan not yet having its adult bill colouration (*see foreground swan on page 106*)

150

Below: Sire, the male parent of a brood.

Right: Cygnet, a young swan.

- **Clear-bill** – an unmarked swan

- **Cygnet** – a newly-hatched or a young swan, derived from both the Latin for swan (Cygnus) and the French for little (suffix -et): it thus literally means 'little swan'. The word appears as 'signet' in historical documents.

- **Dam** – the female parent of a brood

- **Field-bird** – a cygnet whose parents were of doubtful ownership

- **Maiden swan** – one that had not yet nested

- **Sire** – the male parent of a brood

- **Stagg** – a one year old swan

Incidentally, the phrase 'up the swanee', which is generally taken to mean something going wrong, is most likely a reference to the Suwannee river in the southern United States rather than the swan, although like many phrases, there is much uncertainty and debate about its exact origin and meaning.

'A toad wants to eat swan flesh!' is a Chinese phrase for a man who desires a woman who is beyond his status in terms of wealth, social class or beauty.

Many cinemas, hotels and theatres have been named after the swan, especially those associated with William Shakespeare, who lived in Stratford-upon-Avon, where swans feature prominently on the river even to this day.

Companies and organisations have also seen the appeal of using the swan either as a name or as an image or symbol. Swarovski Crystal use a stylised swan as part of their brand, as do Swan Hellenic Cruises, and Swan Vestas matches have been a famous name for many years. Even electrical appliances have turned to the swan to promote their products – Swan was registered as a brand in the early 20th century and is a long-established electrical manufacturer. KLM Royal Dutch Airlines have used an image of a flying swan as part of their business. Sport has also adopted the swan; Swansea City Football Club are known as 'The Swans' and use Cyril The Swan as their mascot.

Below: The elegant, simplified lines of the Swansea City Football Club logo. Naturally, the team's home colours are white.

The swan features significantly as a name or logo in transport, in particular for a variety of aircraft in several countries. The Supermarine Swan was a 1920s British experimental amphibious aircraft (or flying boat) built by Supermarine for maritime reconnaissance. Only one was built and later used for a passenger service between England and France. Hawker also built an ultra-light biplane around the same time, the Cygnet. General Aircraft Limited also used the name Cygnet for a single-engine training aircraft a few years later. The Russian Blackjack supersonic bomber is known as the 'White Swan' by its pilots. The Royal Navy has used the name Swan (or Swann) on at least 20 of its vessels and the name has also been used for sailing ships, and the Australian

The Swan

Navy launched a ship called *HMS Swan* in 1967 – it is now a dive wreck and artificial reef off the coast of Western Australia. The United States Navy has also used *Cygnet* for the name of one of its ships. A steam locomotive in the UK bore the name *Wild Swan* and was used as a cruise train carrying passengers on train journeys which took several days. And cars too have not escaped the influence of the swan – the name *Cygnet* is used by Aston Martin for its small city car.

What designer could hope for a better image than this?

Above, from the left: Coats of Arms for Buckinghamshire County Council, The Worshipful Company of Musicians, and the county shield of Buckinghamshire.

Even plants have been named after the swan. The Monarch butterfly caterpillar only eats plants from the Milkweed (Asclepiadaceae) family – one of these is the Swan Plant (*Asclepias fruticosa*), also known as the Narrow-leaf Cotton Bush. It is so-named because of the shape of the seed pods which have a point that can be likened to the swan's beak, with the pod making up the body. It has hanging bunches of whitish flowers and reaches 4-6 feet in height. Several orchids from the genus Cycnoches have been termed 'swan orchids', because they have slender arching columns of flowers that resemble a swan's neck. They are found in Central America and Amazonia. The word Cycnoches is derived from the Greek words 'kyknos' meaning swan and 'auchen' meaning neck.

There are many place names that use, or have been derived from, the word swan, including towns and cities such as Swansea, Swanage, Swanley and Swanwick; while overseas the word Cygnet has also been used as a place name in this way. In Western Australia, there is the Swan River, famous for its large population of Black swans. Swan Road, Swan Street, Swan Drive and Swan View are popular names for roads in many parts of the world.

In Scandinavia in particular, the swan is highly regarded. The Mute swan is the National Bird of Denmark, and in Finland it is the Whooper swan. In 1985, the swan provided the inspiration for the development of a new symbol of Nordic co-operation. The swan symbol, with its eight quills, represents the five Nordic countries of Denmark, Finland, Iceland, Norway and Sweden, and the three autonomous territories of the Faroe Islands, Greenland and Aland.

Swans are common images on postage stamps. In 1993 a set of five stamps was issued in the UK featuring Abbotsbury Swannery, showing different aspects of the Mute swan lifecycle from egg to adult. Jersey and the Isle of Man have also used images of Mute swans on their stamps. In fact many of the countries where the Mute swan occurs have released stamps featuring the bird. Coins have also been issued which have images of swans on one side or the other; for example, in 2004 Ireland produced a 10 Euro commemorative coin featuring a stylised swan sitting on 10 eggs to celebrate enlargement of the European Union.

The swan has been a common inclusion on Coats of Arms. Originally, these were distinctive designs painted on shields as a means to identify soldiers on the battlefield. The symbols were also embroidered on tunics worn over the armour. Designs were initially fairly simple, but, over the course of time, were added to by subsequent generations wishing to make their mark. As the use of these designs spread, wealthy and high-ranking families started using Coats of Arms for themselves, and eventually the church, towns and cities used them to authenticate documents.

Many of the countries where the Mute swan lives have released stamps featuring the bird.

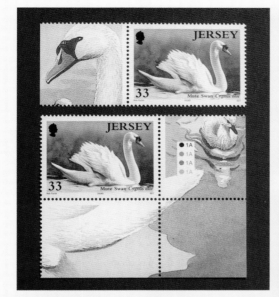

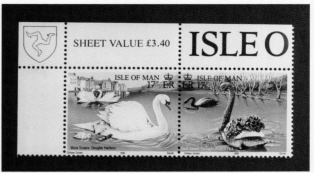

Even today, Coats of Arms are used by a variety of people, cities and institutions and their granting and use is strictly controlled by The College of Arms in London. The presence of a swan would indicate, amongst other things, strength and sincerity, and its wings would imply swiftness and protection. The Coat of Arms of Buckinghamshire County Council, for example, features a white swan in chains. This dates back to the Anglo-Saxon period when swans were bred in Buckinghamshire and it is thought that the chains around the swan's neck indicate that the bird is bound to the Monarch. Buckinghamshire's county flag also features a white swan. The Worshipful Company of Musicians in London also has a swan on its Coat of Arms, as the swan was a symbol of Apollo, God of music. Although Apollo had many animals and birds attributed to him, including the snake, wolf and hawk, it was the swan that symbolised music.

The Cygnus Constellation

From ancient times, civilisations have given names to the patterns of stars in the night sky, in an effort to make recognition and location easier. By linking particular groups of stars together, common names were invented to describe them, with most being named after objects they vaguely resembled, such as a bird or animal. These names are purely subjective, as they are only relevant to the position from which the stars are viewed from earth. Many cultures were dependent on the sky and its features. The position of the stars may have been very useful, for example, in helping farmers know the optimum time for planting crops,

especially in regions where the climatic differentiation in seasons was minimal (different stars and patterns of stars are visible at different times of year).

Cygnus is a large constellation in the northern hemisphere and lies within the Milky Way. It is one of the most easily recognised constellations, and has a long history, being among the 48 constellations listed by Ptolemy in the 2nd century.

The Cygnus constellation was probably named after the swan (cygnus in latin) because of its general resemblance, when its brightest stars are joined together, to a wide-winged long-necked flying bird, but also because of the significance the swan has in history and mythology, and particularly its association with the gods.

One story about how this constellation came to be named relates to two friends, Cygnus and Phaeton, who were racing against each other across the sky. In seeking an advantage, Phaeton unfortunately strayed too close to the sun, his chariot burned, and he fell into a river and died. Despite all his efforts, Cygnus could not reach him at the bottom of the river. He desperately wanted to give his friend a proper burial and begged Zeus to help him. Zeus gave Cygnus a choice: he could assume the body of a swan and dive down deep enough to reach his friend's body, but if he did, he would give up his immortality. Cygnus readily agreed to this, retrieved Phaeton and gave him a proper burial, thus allowing Phaeton's spirit to travel to the afterlife. In honour of this great unselfish act, Zeus placed the image of a swan in the night sky.

Cygnus is one of the favourite constellations of astronomers because of the many shapes, colours and features that it exhibits. It has bright stars, various nebulae, several planets, lots of dust and gas clouds and is relatively easy to see. The central part of the constellation is also known as the Northern Cross.

The main stars are Albireo, Deneb and Sadr. Albireo (or beta Cygni) represents the head of the swan and is a double star with blue and yellow components. The brightest star is Deneb (alpha Cygni): this is at the tail end and is a blue-white supergiant some 200,000 times brighter than our sun. At the centre is Sadr (gamma Cygni) and this is a yellow-white supergiant. There are also other stars in the Cygnus constellation that can be spotted even with the naked eye.

The Cygnus Constellation, visible in the Northern Hemisphere in summer and autumn, and first recorded in the 2nd Century by the astronomer Ptolemy.

CHAPTER TEN

The Swan
& Culture

Universally acknowledged as the most beautiful of the large water birds, swans are revered in many cultures and religions. Great symbolism and meaning has been attached to the swan, which is associated with love, grace and strength and it is also believed to embody the elements of water, air and land. The swan has thus been a source of inspiration for storytellers, artists, musicians and poets since records began. In fact, in virtually every part of the globe, there are stories, legends, fables, myths, folklore, films, poems and music involving the swan, so widespread is its appeal and influence.

Stories

Stories involving swans abound and have been written down over the centuries by virtually all the best-known storytellers, and many other artists besides. Interest is still so strong that many of these stories have been adapted into film, TV, various musical

works and theatre and their popularity shows no sign of abating. Most swan tales have been retold countless times, so some of the details have become lost or altered, but the underlying narrative tends to remain the same. Generally they contain some inherent message relating to the degree of wisdom of individuals. Some of the best-known stories are summarized here:

The Ugly Duckling by Hans Christian Andersen

First published in Denmark in 1843, this is perhaps the best-known story of all about the swan. It tells the story of a cygnet that grows up as part of a family of ducks. He is seen as being very ugly compared to the other ducklings, with his dirty brown feathers and stubby little wings, and soon all the other animals persecute him.

Eventually he decides to run away and fend for himself, managing to survive the harsh winter alone. In the spring, he sees some beautiful white swans gliding on the water and decides to swim over to them. But when he enters the water and sees his reflection, he gets a shock as he sees no longer the ugly grey duckling that he was, but a beautiful white swan, just like the others swimming gracefully out on the water.

This is essentially a story that tells us there is beauty in all things, but that things are not always as they outwardly seem, and that we should not forget to look for inner beauty too.

The Six Swans
by the brothers Grimm

This is another well-known tale, published in Germany in 1812. It is a story about six brothers who were turned into swans by their hateful stepmother and how their sister toils to rescue them from their curse. She must make six shirts out of starwort and not speak or laugh for six long years. But she is plotted against by her husband's evil mother, who eventually has her sentenced to be burned at the stake.

On the day of her execution, she has almost finished making the shirts for her brothers: only the last shirt is missing a left arm. When she is taken to the stake, she brings the shirts with her, and as she is about to be burned, the six years expire and her six brothers, in the form of swans, come flying through the air overhead. She throws the shirts over her brothers and they regain their complete human form, except for the youngest brother, who is left with a swan's wing instead of a left arm, due to the unfinished nature of his shirt. The sister, now free to speak, defends

*It was held that if
you saw three swans
flying together,
it was a sign of
impending disaster.*

herself, and the evil mother is instead burned at the stake, and she and her six brothers live happily ever after.

Aesop's Fables

Aesop was a famous Greek storyteller who lived in the 6th century BC. He is well known for his stories about animals which illustrate the behaviour of people, each teaching a lesson in the form of a moral. Overleaf are a couple of them:

The Swan and The Goose

A rich man bought a swan and a goose in the market one day. He fattened the goose for his table and the swan he kept for its song. When the time came for killing the goose, the cook went to fetch it at night, but unfortunately he was not able to distinguish one bird from the other in the dark. He mistakenly caught the swan and not the goose, and the swan, its life threatened by the cook, burst forth into song and made itself known, thus saving its life by its melodious voice.

The moral of the story: sweet words may deliver us from peril, when harsh words would fail.

The Crow and The Swan

A crow was filled with envy on seeing the beautiful white plumage of the swan. He thought it was due to the water in which the swan constantly swam and bathed. So the crow left the neighbourhood of the sacrificial altars, where he got his living by picking up bits of meat offered in sacrifice, and went and lived amongst the pools and streams. But even though he bathed and washed his feathers many times a day, he could not make them any whiter, and he eventually died of hunger.

The moral of the story: you may change your habits but not your nature.

The Story of The Golden Swan

This is an Indian fable about greed. Buddha was a virtuous householder from Varanasi and worked hard to care for his wife and three daughters. After his death, he was reborn as a golden swan. One day he visited his family in their house, and decided to leave them a golden feather for them to sell and overcome their poverty.

Each year he visited regularly and each time offered them a golden feather, and soon the family overcame their poverty. But his wife was greedy and cruel, and she wanted to be richer much quicker. So she instructed her daughters to catch the swan the next time it visited and to pluck out all its feathers. The daughters were opposed to the plan and warned their mother not to cause the bird any harm. But the next time the golden swan visited, she caught it and plucked out all its feathers.

To her surprise the feathers she plucked out changed to white, because they were plucked against the swan's wishes. The poor bird was in great agony and unable to fly, but the daughters cared for him until he grew new feathers again. He flew away, and never came back.

Left: An unusual cirrus cloud formation in the shape of a swan feather.

171

Beyond reproach: in literature, the swan often symbolizes constancy, nobility and truth.

The Swan
by Roald Dahl

This is a short story about two friends, Ernie and Raymond, who are cruel and who amused themselves by bullying a sensitive boy called Peter. On one occasion they saw a beautiful swan sitting on her nest, and Ernie shoots her. Peter is mortified and he retrieves the poor swan, wishing he could bring her back to life. This gives Ernie an idea – he cuts off the swan's wings and ties them to Peter's arms, then makes him climb a tree and jump from the top to see if he can fly. Suddenly there is a bright light and three people see a great white swan flying high over their village. Meanwhile Peter's mother sees a white thing crash into her garden and she recognises it as her son Peter. She runs over to him, calls an ambulance, and cuts the two great wings of the swan from his arms.

Below; A solitary swan in flight stirs the imagination.

Myths and Legends

Throughout the ages, swans have had an association with the divine, and have often been seen as the physical presence of one of the Gods.

Swans feature significantly in Greek mythology. Perhaps best-known is the story of Leda and The Swan, in which the God Zeus transforms himself into a swan in order to force himself on Leda, Queen of Sparta, resulting in the birth of Helen of Troy. The swan was seen as a powerful symbol of love and beauty: Aphrodite, the Goddess of Love, was said to have ridden a swan and Apollo used swans to draw his chariot across the heavens. The swan also symbolised chastity, another of Aphrodite's qualities, and the birth of Apollo was marked by a flight of circling swans.

Zeus took on the form of a swan in order to ravish Leda.

In Norse mythology, the swan symbolises peace and tranquillity. It tells the story of two swans that drank from the sacred Well of Urdu, at Asgard, the home of the gods, in which the water was so pure that everything that touched it turned white, including the original pair of swans from which all others are descended.

Swan maidens, women able to transform from human to swan and vice-versa, are a common theme in many cultures.

Usually she is temporarily robbed of her powers and must obey or marry a human man. In Germanic mythology, the Valkyries had the power to transform themselves into swans – they were the 12 maidens of Odin, goddesses who presided over wars and granted victory to one side or the other. They were able to cast off their swan plumage and appear to men in human form, but if their plumage was stolen, they were bound to do the bidding of whoever stole it, until it was returned.

In Japanese folklore, the swan was a divine bird that lived in heaven. When all the Ainu people were killed because of war, only one small boy survived. A swan is said to have descended

from heaven and transformed itself into a woman, reared the boy and then married him and had his children, thus preserving the Ainu race.

In Celtic mythology, the swan was associated with growth and fertility. Among the druids, it is said to represent the soul and aid travel to the Other World. Swans were sacred to Celtic poets and musicians, or bards, and their feathers were used to make

The swan is a Celtic symbol of fertility: here, a pair of breeding swans.

the traditional bardic cloaks. Birgit was a Celtic Swan Goddess, who was in charge of wisdom and crafts. The Celts believed that swans were benevolent deities and legend has it that images of swans forged onto silver medallions worn around the neck gave protection to their wearer.

The Irish legend of the Children of Lir is about a mother's jealousy regarding her children's love for one another and their father, and she uses magic to change them into swans for 900 years.

In Hindu mythology, the swan was sacred to Saraswati, the Goddess of Wisdom and Learning, and she sat on a throne made of two swans. The swan is known as the Hamsa bird and signifies the divine mind and the breath of the spirit. People who have attained great spiritual capabilities are sometimes known as Paramahamsa, or 'Great Swan' on account of their ability to travel between various spiritual worlds.

Belief and Superstition

The swan has been very visible in our society for so long that it is not surprising that stories abound about what its presence or behaviour might signify. Most animals have superstitions or stories associated with them and the swan is no exception. And almost everyone is superstitious about something or other.

In many societies, objects or animals can take on specific meaning or association, often based on their appearance or behav-

iour. Such 'totems' can become very important in society and be visibly manifested as objects, signs, rituals or items to be worn. The swan is seen as being strong, graceful, long-lived and pure and was often used as a totem. It is also, certainly in the northern hemisphere, a cold-loving bird and those who had the swan as a totem were said to find it easier to withstand cold climates.

Birds were seen as important symbols in alchemy, the ancient art of using chemicals to try to turn common metals like lead into gold and silver, and to seek an elixir to give eternal life. Alchemists often used bird symbols to aid their experimentation

The swan was an ancient symbol for alchemists.

because they could fly (air was an important element) and therefore had the ability to travel between the earth and the heavens. As a symbol in alchemy, the swan was significant because it was white (thus pure with an inner brightness – souls were often depicted as bright white lights). Because there is no obvious difference between male and female swans (they are the same size and colour), it was seen as neither masculine nor feminine, but instead symbolised hermaphroditism or 'the marriage of opposites', fire and water.

It was also an emblem of mercury, as it was white and very mobile. Paradoxically, in some cultures, the swan was considered to be feminine, and associated with the moon, whilst in others it was masculine, and associated with the sun.

Where do these beliefs come from and might they have some basis in fact? Superstition is defined as an irrational belief 'usually founded on ignorance or fear and characterised by obsessive reverence for omens, charms etc', or 'with regard to the unknown'. Traditional beliefs, knowledge, culture and observations, passed on through generations of families, are likely to have been instrumental in developing superstitions. This could be through a variety of means, such as storytelling, dance, poetry or music. Many people thought that, because birds could fly so high and out of sight, that they regularly flew in and out of heaven and

181

they would have good weather for their voyage.
However, in Australia, people associated the black swan
with shipwrecks, probably because of the general view
that the colour black was seen in a negative context.

- Dreaming of a white swan was said to symbolise
  cleansing and purifying oneself, and also that the
  dreamer would enjoy the company of others.
  Conversely, dreaming about a black swan suggested that
  a deep mystery needed to be unlocked. It was also
  believed by some that dreaming about a white swan
  meant that there would be a death in the family.

- Seeing a swan floating gracefully on still water meant
  that material attainment and wealth was not far away.

- If you met a woman after finding a dead swan, you
  should be very cautious, as she may not be all that
  she seemed.

- Some believed that swans were benevolent deities, and
  that you would be protected if you wore a silver
  medallion stamped with a swan image around your neck.

- Seeing a swan on a Friday morning was said to bring
  good luck; however, if you saw a swan on Friday evening,
  it would bring bad luck.

- If you saw three swans flying together, it was a sign of
  impending disaster.

- Swans were said to contain the souls of people who had
  recently died.

- When a swan lays its head and neck back over its body during the daytime, then a storm is on its way.

- Swans' eggs will only hatch during a storm.

- If a swan took flight, strong winds were to be expected.

- It would bring bad luck if you pointed at a swan.

- If a man killed a swan, he would die within a year.

- If a man robbed a swan's nest, the swan would bring fire and burn down his house.

- Finally, it is a widely-held myth that a swan is capable of breaking a man's arm. It couldn't.

Art, Poetry and Music

The prevalence of the swan as a theme in mythology, folklore and story-telling led quite logically to it also being one of the most popular subjects in the arts. Rock carvings and cave paintings of swans have been found dating back to Stone Age times, and swans continue to be a source of inspiration for all types of artistic works around the world.

Many paintings and sculptures featuring swans have been produced throughout the course of history, including some by celebrated artists such as Michelangelo, Cézanne and Dante. The modern day classic *Swans Reflecting Elephants* was painted in 1937 by the Spanish artist Salvador Dali – it is one of his famous double images, as visual illusion was a major part of Dali's philosophy. In this painting, three swans in front of bleak featureless trees are reflected in a lake so that their heads become the heads of elephants and the trees become the elephants' bodies.

Take-off: a Mute swan runs across the surface of the water.

Poets have enthused about the beauty and grace of the swan. Numerous poems have been written over the centuries, perhaps the most famous being *The Wild Swans at Coole* by W. B. Yeats written in 1919, which includes the lines:

I have looked upon those brilliant creatures,

And now my heart is sore.

All's changed since I, hearing at twilight,

The first time on this shore,

The bell-beat of their wings above my head,

Trod with a lighter tread.

Unwearied still, lover by lover,

They paddle in the cold

Companionable streams or climb the air;

Their hearts have not grown old;

Passion or conquest, wander where they will,

Attend upon them still.

But now they drift on the still water,

Mysterious, beautiful;

Among what rushes will they build,

By what lakes edge or pool

Delight men's eyes when I awake some day

To find they have flown away?

William Shakespeare, widely regarded as the best playwright of the western world, was also an actor and a poet and has been affectionately given the epithet 'The Sweet Swan of Avon', probably because of the great popularity of his works and the fact that swans have been a feature of Stratford-upon-Avon, his place of birth and death, for such a long time.

Alfred Lord Tennyson also wrote about the swan, most splendidly in his evocative poem *The Dying Swan*. The Russian ballerina Anna Pavlova was thought to have been inspired to work on the famous ballet of the same name after reading the poem.

Apollo was the Greek God of Music, and his soul is said to have passed into the body of a swan when he died. This may also provide one explanation for the expression 'swansong' – the belief that swans sing when they are dying. Orpheus, the son of Apollo, was held to be one of the greatest musicians in ancient Greece. It was said that he could charm the birds and animals with his singing, and when he died, his soul also changed into a swan. The Worshipful Company of Musicians in London has a swan on its Coat of Arms, perhaps for these reasons.

Reference to the seven swans a-swimming in the popular carol *The Twelve Days of Christmas* is thought by some to represent the seven sacraments of Catholicism, but it is just as likely to be simply a reflection of the swan's valuable status in society. Swans were seen as beautiful creatures, a source of feathers for down and decoration, a possible choice for Christmas dinner etc and so there were many reasons to consider them as a generous Christmas gift.

Even popular music has turned to the swan for inspiration, as in Marc Bolan's *Ride a White Swan* by the pop group T Rex.

The swan has often featured as a theme in ballet, opera and orchestral music. The world-famous ballet *Swan Lake*, with music composed by Tchaikovsky, tells the story of Odette, a princess turned into a swan by an evil sorcerer's curse. The swan appears in operatic works such as Parsifal, in which a swan is slain, and in the romantic Lohengrin, both by the German composer Richard Wagner. The Finnish composer Jean Sibelius wrote a piece of music called *The Swan of Tuonela*, designed for a small orchestra in which the cor anglais plays the voice of the swan. In it a mystical swan swims around Tuonela, the island of the dead. *The Swan* is a short musical composition for cello and piano from Saint Saens' *Carnival of the Animals*.

CHAPTER ELEVEN

Swans & the Law

The swan became a valuable commodity for a variety of reasons, most notably as a source of food and a symbol of status in society. Prior to the 15th century, ownership was supposedly only granted by the Crown, but this seemed to have been largely ignored, so that anyone who could acquire Mute swans (often unscrupulously) and retain them, did so.

Such ownership was widespread and different geographical regions gradually established a variety of written and unwritten customs and rules about owning and trading in swans. However, because of the bird's value and its ability to confer high social status on its owner, it is not surprising that there were frequent altercations between landowners, disputes with the Crown, instances of theft and illegal killing of birds, the stealing of eggs or the deliberate (and sometimes accidental) damaging of nests.

Ownership of swans was taken so seriously that special Swanning Courts (Courts of Swan-mote) were established to deal with such incidents. These courts had the power to draw up additional rules affecting swan-keeping in their area if they were needed, provided that they did not conflict with existing rules. Historical records show that, despite these courts, the stealing of both birds and their eggs was rife, and this led to the need for more robust mechanisms to be put in place to deal with the crimes. Various Commissions were established to consider such cases and to administer appropriate punishment.

The two most important Commissions were set up in 1463, one for the River Thames area and the other for the Fenland area, these being the largest swan-keeping regions in the country. They were charged with examining all the irregular practices surrounding swan ownership, and their findings essentially led to the 1482 *Act of Swans*. As well as specifying how swans should be kept, one of the more important features of this Act was to restrict ownership to wealthy landowners, thus depriving everyone of the right to own swans, and therefore reinforcing the swan's value as a status symbol.

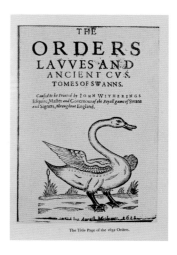

The Title Page of the 1632 Orders.

Severe and detailed laws were passed concerning the theft and damage of swans.

Over subsequent years, additional local laws (or Orders) were developed which further protected the swan, for example, by making it illegal to kill them with bows, guns or dogs, and protecting swans at the nest. Various, and often severe, penalties were set for breaking these laws, such as imprisonment for a year and a day for stealing an egg.

Above: Highly vulnerable at this stage, cygnets rely on strength in numbers, the vigilance of their parents, and any laws which protect them from the detrimental attentions of the general public.

The 1482 *Act of Swans* and several subsequent Acts were eventually abolished with the 1831 *Game Act*. Although this Act primarily applied to game birds such as grouse and pheasant, it also made provision for the protection of swans. The *Protection of Birds Act* in 1954 offered further protection to all wild birds.

Nowadays the primary legislation protecting birds in England and Wales is the *Wildlife and Countryside Act* of 1981. The basic principle of this Act is that all wild birds, their nests and eggs are protected by law (although there are a few exceptions relating to game birds and some wildfowl).

The Swan

The law states that it is an offence to:

- intentionally kill, injure or take a wild bird.

- intentionally take, damage or destroy the nest of any wild bird whilst it is in use or being built.

- intentionally take or destroy the egg of any wild bird.

- have in one's possession or control any wild bird, dead or alive, or any part of a wild bird, which has been taken in contravention of the Act or the *Protection of Birds Act* 1954.

A swan stretches its powerful wings.

- have in one's possession or control any egg or part of an egg which has been taken in contravention of the Act or the *Protection of Birds Act* 1954.

- use traps or similar items to kill, injure or take wild birds.

The maximum penalty that can be imposed for an offence under this Act – in respect of each single bird, nest or egg – is a fine of up to £5,000 and/or six months' imprisonment.

So the *Wildlife and Countryside Act* now protects all swans, and the Queen still technically owns all the swans in Great Britain, except for those in the Orkney Islands where swans belong to the people. This is because the Vikings who settled in the Orkney Islands brought with them their own Norse system of inheritance and law (called Udal Law) which states that the swan is the property of the people rather than the Crown, and the principles of this law still apply today. However, the *Wildlife and Countryside Act* applies in the Orkney Islands as well, which limits the rights of the people of the Orkney Islands to watching swans, but not killing or eating them.

In Scotland, the *Nature Conservation Act* 2004 imposes a wide-ranging responsibility on the people of Scotland to conserve and protect their natural heritage.

CHAPTER TWELVE

Saving our Swans

Because there are relatively large numbers of swans in our countryside (and indeed in our towns) that are easy to see, we tend to think that they are flourishing and in little need of any help from us. From a conservation point of view, their status is classified as being of 'least concern' because of their wide range and stable population. But there are considerable pressures on their existence, primarily because of the endless march of human civilisation and all that brings with it.

Swans have few natural enemies but sadly many unnatural ones – thousands of them are harassed, attacked, poisoned and shot every year. Fortunately there is substantial public interest and support for swans and various bodies are actively involved in their conservation, so the future looks promising and we should continue to see and admire these beautiful birds for years to come.

The Dangers Facing Swans

Like other wildlife, swans are not immune to the effects of urbanisation and consequent habitat loss. The building of new towns and cities, roads, railways and other structures that eat away at our natural environment inevitably means that space suitable for our wildlife is constantly shrinking. Even Green Belt land, which should be sacrosanct, is under pressure for building the increasing number of houses that we seem to need. Rivers, lakes and ponds disappear or are significantly affected so that they become unsuitable for breeding birds. Increasing amounts of water are being taken out of the environment to service the needs of the human population, amounts that cannot realistically be sustained in the long term.

Increasing urbanisation results in increasing waste, and inevitably some of this finds its way into the environment. Pollution of our waterways has a detrimental effect on our wildlife, but this may take a while to be noticed in the swan population as it is at the top of the food-chain. Poisoning due to oil spillage, both domestic

Lack of water due to building threatens the habitat of the Mute swan.

and industrial, continues to be a major hazard for swans. Fortunately, the quality of our main waterways is monitored to ensure that any pollution is minimised, and if pollution does occur, it can be rapidly identified and dealt with. But unfortunately instances of mass death due to poisoning sometimes still occur.

Right: Injured swans recovering at the Swan Sanctuary in Middlesex.

Lead poisoning is perhaps the most familiar example of poisoning of swans. During the 1960s, the number of swans decreased dramatically in some areas of the country, and investigations revealed that most of the birds were dying of lead poisoning. Many of the swans examined contained lead weights, discarded by anglers, in their gizzards. This is picked up when they deliberately ingest grit and small stones to grind down their food. The ground lead is then easily absorbed into the bloodstream, causing

the bird's muscles to weaken and they eventually die. Typical signs of lead poisoning include swans with a kinked neck, as the muscles are unable to hold the neck up correctly.

The subsequent banning of the use of lead weights saw a recovery in swan numbers, although some deaths still occur due to the ingestion of residual lead in river silt. In fact, it is thought

A perfect place for a swan to nest, but it could soon be disturbed by noise or water-sports and will abandon its eggs if necessary.

that there is so much discarded lead in our waterways that the problem of lead poisoning in swans may never go away. Ingestion of discarded lead shot from shooting can also result in lead poisoning. It is suspected that lower levels of lead poisoning may contribute to deaths caused by flying accidents as the bird's agility and eyesight may be affected. The *Environmental Protection Regulations* 1999 in the UK banned the use of lead shot for the shooting of ducks, geese and swans, but in many countries lead is still widely used as there is no preventative legislation in place.

Increasing use of water by the human population and longer, drier summers can cause lower water levels in rivers and lakes, allowing swans to reach further down to sediments which may contain harmful materials such as lead and bacteria.

The increase in popularity of water sports can have a significant impact on aquatic wildlife. Human activity can affect both the birds themselves and their environment. Activities that have the most effect are generally those involving powered watercraft, such as water-skiing, jet-skiing and speedboats, as these can create substantial noise and disturbance to the water surface. Waves can erode water margins and banks and may also damage or flood nests that are close to the water level.

Excessive noise can cause the swans distress, leading them to abandon their nests. Even if they leave the nest only temporarily, this can result in problems such as egg mortality (eggs can become cold and die if they are left exposed) and an increase in egg or chick predation. The swans can also be affected if the disturbance is in their favourite, or particularly productive, feeding areas. Seasonal restrictions, speed limitations and the use of permits are some of the controls that are being used to help the wildlife in such areas. Even shoreline activities such as walking, bird watching and fishing can be damaging to wildlife, especially if these generate a high level of noise.

The discarding or loss of fishing hooks and lengths of nylon fishing line are a real hazard to swans and they can easily become entangled. Hooks can become caught in the mouth, tongue and even the throat. These injuries can be extremely painful and can significantly affect a swan's ability to feed. Swans with hook injuries often look emaciated and lethargic and can quickly die if not treated. Fishing line can cause more extensive injuries as it can

A shocking contrast between the pure white of the swan and the colourful debris of its nest.

Above: Mink bites on a swan.

Below: Discarded wire and fishing line can cause terrible injuries.

become wrapped around the bird, and can, over time, cause deep wounds which subsequently become infected. Unfortunately most fishing lines are not bio-degradable.

After fishing tackle injuries, the primary cause of injury and fatality in our Mute swan population is, very sadly, due to wildlife vandalism. This is especially true during the moult and during the breeding season when the birds cannot, or are reluctant to, fly away. And unfortunately, the number of attacks show little sign of decreasing, judging by the number of reports appearing in the national press and statistics from swan conservation bodies.

Swans are frequently fed by the general public and, as a result, they have become more trusting of people and easy to approach, making them a soft target for vandals. Over the years there have been some horrific attacks on our swan population by mindless individuals, for example:

- deliberately shooting birds with air rifles and crossbows
- the use of catapults, and the throwing of stones and bricks, at birds sitting on the nest

- the destruction of nests and the stealing of eggs

- attacks by uncontrolled dogs

- the deliberate release of oil into waterways

- deliberately driving vehicles at the birds in order to injure or kill them

In one particularly cruel and appalling attack, a young swan was fed a lit firework concealed in a piece of bread: needless to say, the poor bird suffered horrific injuries and had to be put down humanely by a vet.

The thoughtless discarding of litter such as plastic bags and broken glass can also cause significant harm and death to swans.

Even if the birds survive such attacks, the injuries sustained invariably cause the birds considerable trauma and unnecessary suffering. Should the individuals responsible for such barbaric attacks be identified and prosecuted, the conviction rate is very low and justice is seldom dispensed.

Not content with harassing and injuring the birds, some elements of our society today have been accused of killing swans for food, resulting in such appalling headlines in the press as *Slaughter of the Swans*. Humans are still the biggest factor in the decline of our swan population.

The swan's omnivorous diet has occasionally led it into conflict with farmers. There are several well-publicised cases of swans causing substantial damage and economic loss to crops, such as watercress and oilseed rape, resulting in the birds being labelled as pests and vermin. A flock can cause significant damage, as much through trampling with their large feet as by direct consumption, and each bird can eat several kilograms of vegetation each day. Most damage occurs during the late winter and early spring, when the swan's natural food is at its scarcest. In such circumstances the relationship between farming communities and bird conservation groups can become strained and it is difficult to find ways of resolving this. In some cases, compensation payments may be possible, or agreement reached about the

A vulnerable time for the swan family.

that the birds are able to swallow water with their food. Feeding the birds on land is environmentally unsound as it encourages them to leave the safety of the water when they see people and causes unnaturally large congregations. Too much carbohydrate in the diet also leads to an increase in defecation and this can cause an increase in disease-producing bacteria that can be harmful to both birds and humans. Birds will naturally seek out easy sources of food and such a dependence on people for food can have a detrimental effect on swan behaviour. Young swans, for example, may not learn to forage naturally and may lose their natural fear and become more aggressive.

Conservation

Thousands of swans are injured each year. Fortunately there are many swan conservation organisations which provide help.

Swan rescue groups and charities

These provide care and treatment for sick and injured swans, and include organisations such as Swan Lifeline (the oldest registered charity for swans) and The Swan Sanctuary in Middlesex, the largest completely self-contained swan hospital in the UK. They are available 24 hours a day, seven days a week, to provide distressed swans with treatment in the field or back at their sanctuaries. Swans are treated and monitored under close

Swan ambulances from the Swan Sanctuary.

Above: The Swan Sanctuary logo.

supervision until their condition improves, when they can then be placed in outdoor rehabilitation areas and ultimately returned to the wild. These organisations have advanced facilities and equipment including operating theatres to enable them to carry out complex surgery when needed.

Sometimes severely injured or disabled birds are unable to look after themselves in the wild and these birds are re-homed in safe waters (where food and protection from natural predators is provided) to live out the rest of their days in peace. There is a constant need for these safe havens.

Because of their extensive experience in helping injured birds, these organisations are well-placed to develop codes of best practice, to share information and to standardize their activities throughout the country (such as how best to capture and transport injured swans). Collating information about rescued swans is also important in identifying common problems.

Swan rescue groups also undertake the temporary relocation of birds from lakes or rivers when needed, such as when watersports events (such as the Henley rowing regatta on the River Thames) take place, or when lakes are being cleaned or dredged.

Education and training emanating from these swan centres is important and can be given to various groups including the general public, students, other rescue organisations and the emergency services which might come into contact with swans needing help.

The annual Swan Upping on the River Thames is now essentially a conservation activity, supported by bodies including the Crown, the Vintners and the Dyers Livery Companies in London and various academic institutions. This annual swan census helps to monitor the number and condition of the Mute swans on the Thames, and is a visible conservation effort that the public can witness first-hand. The Vintners' Company is the trustee of *Save Our Swans*, an established Trust founded to assist in the welfare of sick and injured swans on the River Thames.

These organisations are dependent on charitable donations, fund-raising activities and in particular the work of volunteers.

Bird Conservation Organisations

These are involved in conservation and research of birds in general, and work with swans and the various swan rescue groups forms only a part of their activities. They include well-known organisations such as the RSPB (The Royal Society for the Protection of Birds), the British Trust for Ornithology (BTO) and Birdlife International.

Research and monitoring forms a large part of swan conservation work, and the better we can understand the biology, behaviour and habitat needs of birds, the better we will know how best to help and conserve them. Work on identifying the causes of significant population changes, both decreases and increases, is especially important.

The first Mute swan census was undertaken in 1955 and the numbers of swans have been counted periodically ever since. Current research programmes include looking at ways of reducing the amount of lead that finds its way into the environment, and how best to protect crops from bird damage. They are also well placed to look at the interaction between bird species, for example, the possible use of swans to help reduce the number of Canada geese, which have reached pest proportions in some areas. Swans are very territorial and will drive other large birds, particularly geese, away from lakes and stretches of river during the breeding season.

Most swans in the UK will have a ring (or band) of aluminium or other lightweight material on one of their legs. This bird ringing is an invaluable tool in helping to study swans. Usually, the right leg is tagged for males and the left for females. Each ring has a unique code that shows when and where the bird was originally caught and who to contact should the bird be found again. The information on the ring is often conspicuous so that the details can be read from afar (for example through binoculars) without having to recapture the swan. The rings are very light and do not cause the swans any distress or affect their behaviour. Data gathered from ringed birds can provide useful information on topics such as migration and feeding patterns, longevity and territorial behaviour.

Conservation isn't just about increasing numbers, but about finding a population level that the environment can sustain, taking into account the habitat and other wildlife that may be present.

For example, too many swans in an area might result in an unnatural decrease in the submerged vegetation and hence negatively affect other aquatic life such as insect larvae, crustaceans and fish.

The increase in popularity of fishing has led to an increase in the amount of tackle discarded in lakes and rivers, therefore it is critically important to liaise with angling groups to find mutually agreeable ways of addressing this problem.

With increasing urbanisation, habitat loss for swans is a major concern and conservation groups work hard to identify, purchase and protect important wildlife areas, often being instrumental in the creation of new nature reserves.

Another important part of swan conservation work is to help educate the general public about the birds, their needs, the effects our society has on them and how they can help.

Wildlife Organisations

A number of other wildlife and environmental organisations also have an interest in the well-being of swans.

The Wildfowl and Wetlands Trust (WWT) is a leading UK conservation organisation saving wetlands for both wildlife and people across the world. It is a charity founded in 1946 by the naturalist Sir Peter Scott. It is well-known for its work with swans, especially Bewick's and Whooper swans, and now has a national network of wetland sites that can be visited. This is especially important

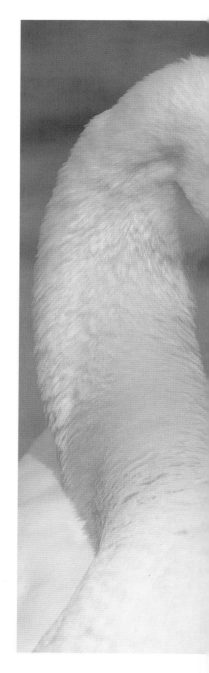

as it provides opportunities for people to see our wildlife at close quarters. More than half of the world's wetlands have been lost over the past century and the WWT plays a major role in helping to protect these essential eco-systems and to create new ones where it is possible and appropriate to do so.

Sir Peter Scott was also a founder member of the **World Wildlife Fund**, now called simply **WWF**, which has the famous Giant Panda as its logo. Founded in 1961 in Switzerland, it works on a global basis to help conserve the world's natural resources. It continues to lobby governments, industry and policy makers, it funds many international conservation projects, and is especially concerned with the wider implications of Man's activities on the environment. It was closely concerned, for example, with the investigation into the devastation of what was probably the world's largest population of black-necked swans in South America due to industrial pollution.

Defra is the UK government department responsible for policy and regulations on the environment, food and rural affairs. They undertake activities and research on a variety of environmental and wildlife projects, particularly those crossing various disciplines; one of their projects, for example, looked at developing a cost-effective alternative to shooting swans that cause significant crop damage, by utilising brightly coloured tape and twine.

The Royal Society for the Prevention of Cruelty to Animals (RSPCA) has been in existence since 1824 and is often called upon to help rescue injured swans. It liaises very closely with swan rescue centres.

Natural England is the government's advisor on the natural environment and its responsibilities include managing nature reserves and designating national parks and areas of outstanding natural beauty. They are involved in projects relating to all three of our swan species.

SWAN is the acronym for the **Society for Wildlife and Nature**, an international organisation dedicated to worldwide conservation. Originally established in Taiwan in the early 1980s, it now has offices in various countries including Australia and Japan. It is concerned with the conservation, study and cultivation of wild animals and plants, environmental pollution, and international cooperation.

Given the swan's global appeal, it is not surprising that there are many other international groups, charities and organisations concerned with the welfare of swans. International meetings and symposia dedicated to swan conservation take place periodically in various parts of the world, discussing a wide range of topics relating to the world's swans.

These activities, from a great variety of sources, illustrate the huge amount of work undertaken to conserve not just Mute swans, but all of the world's swan species. Work covers monitoring, research, education, communication, law-making, land purchase, habitat creation and management – all of which requires dialogue, negotiation and agreement with governments, industry, individuals, conservation groups and other charities. It is an expensive, potentially complicated and time-consuming task. Inevitably conflicts between the various parties with differing interests and priorities do sometimes occur. It is a positive sign that all these efforts are being undertaken, but also a sad reflection of the negative impact we have had on our wildlife that this work is so essential. It is not all doom and gloom, however: increasing public awareness and interest, better water quality, the creation of suitable breeding sites (such as gravel pits), and milder winters have helped swan numbers remain relatively stable.

Sponsor a Swan

at The Swan Sanctuary, Shepperton

The Sponsor–a–Swan scheme is one of the main sources of income for The Swan Sanctuary. It helps to pay for the day-to-day running-expenses such as food and veterinary bills and it costs from £12 per swan. Sponsors receive details about their allotted swan(s) and regular newsletters detailing the latest information about the Sanctuary and its work throughout the year.

Further details:
www.theswansanctuary.org.uk/sponsorship.php

Index

Act of Swans 1482   10, 193
Air sac system   49
Arrows   135
Art   186-9
Bathing   75-7
Beak   49, 69
Bewick's swan   22
Biology   39
Black swan   21
Black-necked swan   21
Breeding   83-7
Busking   35, 87
Carpal bone   86
Charities   210-12
Coats of Arms   157
Cob   39
Communication   112-3
Conservation   199-217
Constellation, Cygnus   160-3
Coscoroba swan   23-4
Courtship   90-5
Cygnets   99-106
Cygnus, constellation   160-3
Dabbling   107
Digestion   72
Diseases   120-3
Disputes, territorial   88-9
Distribution   13-18
Domestication   125-132
Down   48, 136
Dyers   139
Eating   132-3
Eggs   96-8

Enemies   117-123
Excretion   72
Eyes   49, 63-8
Feathers   46
Feeding   107-110
Fletching   135
Flight   51-4
Fossil, swan   26
Gibbons, Orlando   6
Gizzard   73
Hatching   99-103
Hearing   56
Heart   49
Incubation   96-8
Knob   70
Lifespan   39
Literature and swans   165-74
Livery companies   139
Marking swans   130-1
Mating   90-5
Migration   51
Moult   81
Music   186-9
Myths and legends   175-9
Nature Conservation Act 2004   197
Navigation   51
Neck   41
Nest   96-8
Nictitating membrane   66
Parasites   123
Pen   39
Phallus   73
Poetry   186-9

Left: Passing swans pause to feed on the sea at Penzance.

Index

Polish swan	20	Superstitions	179-185
Preen gland	46	Swan-goose	25
Preening	78-80	Swan, evolution	25
Protection of Birds Act 1954	193, 197	Swansea City AFC	155
Pub signs	153	Syrinx	59
Queen's Swan Marker	145	Territory	88
Queen's Swan Uppers	140	Testicles	49
Queen's Swan Warden	140	third eyelid	66
Quill pen	134-5	Trumpeter swan	22
Royal connection	35	Tundra swan	22
Sanctuary, Swan, Middlesex		Ugly Duckling	167
	201, 208, 210, 211	Upping, Swan	139-145
Seawater	70	Vintners	139
Skeleton	41-4	Whistling swan	22
Sleep, rest	81-2	Whooper swan	21
Species	19-25	*Wildlife & Countryside Act* 1981	193,197
Sponsor a Swan	219	Wingspan	39
Stamps	158-9